THE
FABULOUS
MANAGER

THE FABULOUS MANAGER

20 Key Lessons Towards Management Excellence

KENNETH STOTT   **ALLAN WALKER**

PRENTICE HALL

New York London Toronto Sydney Tokyo Singapore

First published 1994 by
Prentice Hall
Simon & Schuster (Asia) Pte Ltd
Alexandra Distripark
Block 4, #04-31
Pasir Panjang Road
Singapore 0511

Cover photograph by The Image Bank

Printed in Singapore

1 2 3 4 5   98 97 96 95 94

ISBN 0-13-296550-X

Prentice Hall International (UK) Limited, London
Prentice Hall of Australia Pty. Limited, Sydney
Prentice Hall Canada Inc., Toronto
Prentice Hall Hispanoamericana, S.A., Mexico
Prentice Hall of India Private Limited, New Delhi
Prentice Hall of Japan, Inc., Tokyo
Editora Prentice Hall do Brasil, Ltda., Rio de Janeiro
Prentice Hall, Inc., Englewood Cliffs, New Jersey

Contents

Preface   ix

Introduction   1

1 What We Can Learn From Bad Managers   7

The 'We have always done it this way' manager 8
The 'Wisdom in high places only' manager 10
The 'It can't be done here' manager 11
The 'That's a great idea' manager 11
The 'Me first' manager 12   ◆   The 'Zookeeper' manager 12
The 'Spy' manager 13   ◆   The 'Anointed' manager 13

2 What Makes You a Good Manager?   17

A simple question 17   ◆   It all depends . . . 18
A manager or a leader? 19   ◆   People are important 19
Two major considerations 19   ◆   What makes a good manager? 20
What are the right things? 20   ◆   Striking a balance 21
Can you be good at everything? 21

3 The Manager As Developer: Improving Your Workers   25

A satisfied workforce 26   ◆   Self-development 26
Individual employee development 27   ◆   Team development 28
Training or development? 28
What does development mean in practice? 29

4 Sharing Power With Your People   **31**

The traditional picture 31 ◆ Empowerment 32
The leader's role in empowerment 33 ◆ Understanding and valuing 34
Giving direction 35 ◆ Working together 35
Giving the power to act 35 ◆ Assigning those tasks 36
Making that input real 36 ◆ Surrendering some control 37
Taking risks 37

5 Leadership: It's More Than Who You Are   **39**

Easy images 40 ◆ He was born like that 41
He has more paper 41 ◆ You are what you are – aren't you? 41
It worked at my place – how about yours? 42
Task-centred or people-centred? 43 ◆ Changing your style 43
Action leaders 44 ◆ Getting it together 45

6 Motivation Means More Than Money   **47**

They're not all the same 49 ◆ Giving people challenge 50
Making their input meaningful 50 ◆ I did it! 51 ◆ I can do that 51
Tools to do the job 52 ◆ Growth is important 53
What are your expectations? 53

7 Who Makes the Decisions Around Here?   **57**

Are all decisions the same? 58 ◆ Everyday decisions 58
Crisis decisions 59 ◆ Deep decisions 59 ◆ Know-how 60
Can they live with it? 61 ◆ How good is it? 61
How long have you got? 62 ◆ Why, in my day . . . 62
That's how we do things around here 63

8 Delegating or Dishing Out Work?   **65**

Tartonia loses her head 65 ◆ Sang Nila loses some friends 67
What real delegation is 67 ◆ It isn't easy 68
Some critical questions 68 ◆ Doing it right 69
Think 69 ◆ Prepare 69 ◆ Select 70 ◆ Meet 70
Contract 71 ◆ Monitor 71 ◆ Review 72

9 Ruining or Developing Teamwork: Take Your Choice   **75**

How to ruin teamwork in thirteen easy lessons 75 ◆ Development 77
Shared targets 77 ◆ Quality relationships 78 ◆ Pulling together 79
Balanced leadership 81 ◆ Building winning teams 81

10 Successful Teams: Getting the Right People   83

Roles 83 ♦ Unbalanced teams 85
How to create a balanced team 86

11 Making Appraisal Worthwhile   89

Are you really open? 89 ♦ Questionable practices 91
Should appraisal be linked to pay? 91 ♦ Let's look forward 92
How do you make the most of people's potential? 92
A partnership 92 ♦ Seeing appraisal as an opportunity 93
Using appraisal to build on strengths 93 ♦ Words and action 93
How to do it 94 ♦ Getting the appraisal interview right 94
Using appraisal to transform performance 95

12 Selecting the Right Person: The Art of Interviewing   97

What is the purpose of interviewing? 97
What can you do to make interviews lousy? 98
How to make interviews work well 98 ♦ The interview itself 99
What are the most common interviewing problems? 101
How to ask telling questions 101
The types of questions you should avoid 102
Setting up interviews 103
What should you cover in selection interviews? 104

13 Reach Agreement and Everyone Is Happy!   107

Do you always have to negotiate? 109 ♦ How does negotiation work? 109
What do you need to prepare before negotiating? 110
How do you start the negotiation off? 111 ♦ What next? 112
What happens if you can't agree? 112
How to get 'super' agreements 113
Some miscellaneous (or mischievous) negotiation tactics 114

14 How to Get Your Way Without Being Bossy: The Skilful Influencer   115

Is the boss a bully? 115 ♦ Things are different now 116
How do some managers seem to get their way? 116
Why do some not do so well? 116
Using muscle as a last resort 116
How can you have your way but still maintain relationships? 117
Getting it right 120 ♦ Have you chosen the right strategy? 121
How do you become a successful influencer? 121
Better still, how do you become an 'expert' influencer? 122

15 Getting Ready for the Weekly Pow-wow 125

Poor meetings 125 ◆ Meeting Joan 127 ◆ Be prepared 128

16 Getting to Grips With Conflict 133

How fights start 133 ◆ Positive or negative conflict 135
Turn the other way 135 ◆ Do what you like 136 ◆ Stop it 137
Meet you half way 137 ◆ Let's work together 137

17 Attacks By Time Thieves: How to Defend Yourself 141

Outside and inside thieves 141 ◆ Let's do it later 142
That's not good enough 143 ◆ You never told me 144
Interrupt me, please 145 ◆ Lock them up 146

18 Writing Management Reports 149

How to get ready to write the report 150
Getting the message across 151 ◆ What should the report look like? 151
What is the best style to use? 151 ◆ How to make your report clear 152
How to lay out your report 153
What is there to do when it's finished? 154
How to sharpen your report even more 154
Does your report make sense? 155

19 Presenting Your Ideas in Public 157

Doing your homework 158
How do you give your presentation shape? 160
How do you make the presentation work well? 162
What type of presenter are you? 163

20 Management Structure: Getting It Right 165

Do they always work out as planned? 165
Putting the pieces together 167
Matching the structure with what you are trying to do 167
Complicated or outdated structures 168 ◆ Getting it right 168
What sort of structure can you have? 168 ◆ Go for simplicity 170
Getting the best of both worlds 170
What can you do to improve matters? 170 ◆ Start small 171
Accept that things have to change 171

Conclusion 173

Index 177

Preface

If there is one good thing about writing a book for busy practising managers, it is that you have to clarify your thoughts and make sense of a bewildering array of information from the management literature. Of course, the temptation for some authors is to go the other way and present ideas and concepts too simplistically. That way, the ideas lose their substance.

What we have tried to do is to give you some sound, proven principles to work on, and we have selected those concepts which we believe are the most important in transforming your managerial performance – to make you a 'fabulous' manager. We have also tried to eliminate much of the coma-inducing jargon you have to wade through in textbooks.

We hope we have succeeded and that you find our fayre acceptable. We have not succeeded, however, in finding an alternative to the male pronoun, and we apologise to those who gnash their teeth at the sight of 'he', 'him' and 'his' in every other sentence. Our attempts to change this were hopelessly clumsy.

Some readers may recognise some of our chapters if they have read our work in other sources. Indeed, the reaction to our *Business Times* articles and those in several management magazines was encouragingly favourable, and we felt impelled to put together a collection which would cover what we consider to be the key issues in management.

One confession we have to make is that the humorous interpolations are not our own. We would certainly like to lay claim to many of the anecdotes, but we have been largely influenced by the stories friends have told us and the material we have read in various books, rather than by our own imaginations.

Unlike our policy in other books, we have decided not to break up this text by inserting references. Indeed, we don't even recall where some of the references came from. We can only tell you about several texts that have given us material and raised more than the odd chuckle. And if you want to enjoy the funny side of life, we can do no better than recommend these splendid books for your bedtime reading.

First, *The Solid Singapore Joke Book*. Ben Mathews is a master when it comes to humour. His book, a little saucy in places, is an absolute delight. *Braude's Treasury of Wit and Humor for All Occasions* too covers all the subjects under the sun, and has something to say for every occasion. If you are a regular public speaker, these books will serve you well.

The best favour our Singaporean friend did for us was to introduce us to the work of Anthony de Mello. He relates jokes, yes, but his stories are full of profound meaning, and if you want to enjoy a sometimes irreverent, but always humorous look at life, the late de Mello's *Prayer of the Frog*, Volumes 1 and 2 are well worth the investment. We are indeed indebted to the creators of all the above texts for the inspiration and material for our humble volume. We are also grateful to Jerene Tan and Ang Lee Ming at Prentice Hall in Singapore for their unceasing support, and to Doug McGufficke in Australia for his help in keeping us up to date with developments in Belbin's team roles work. We would also mention former colleagues who have given us encouragement to continue writing and who have used our books in their lecturing. In particular, Dr Narendra Dixit and Dr Zhang Yenming deserve a special mention. Last, but not least, we thank Andrea and Kim for being the guinea pigs for our sometimes bizarre sense of humour. To all, we give our thanks.

Kenneth Stott
Allan Walker

Acknowledgements

Acknowledgement is made to the following sources for permission to adapt in this book previously published material:

The Prayer of the Frog, Volumes 1 and 2, by A. De Mello, 1989, Gujarat Sahitya Prakash, Gujarat, India.

Braude's Treasury of Wit & Humor for All Occasions, Revised Edition, by Jacob M. Braude, Revisor Glenn Van Ekeren, © 1991, used by permission of the publisher, Prentice Hall/A division of Simon & Schuster, Englewood Cliffs, NJ.

The Solid Singapore Joke Book, by Ben Mathews, 1990, with permission from Flame of the Forest Pte Ltd, Singapore.

Introduction

This is the book many managers and colleagues have been pressing us to write for some time – honestly! Having found *Making Management Work* useful, these people were asking for a text that would draw out the main points and be 'portable' (*Making Management Work* was far from that!). They wanted something they could read on the bus, train, or over lunch.

So here it is. But in writing it, we have done much more than simply condense the learning points from our earlier books. We have listened intently to the questions our management friends have been asking. What do they really want to know? What troubles them? What things keep cropping up time and time again?

Plenty of Questions

The more discussions we had with practising managers, the more questions emerged. While we had to read between the lines occasionally, those below are just some of the concerns expressed:

- How can I make more time? I know I am not doing half the things I should be doing.
- Should I share decisions with my workers?
- What if they make a bad decision?
- How can I get my staff motivated?
- How can I get them working together like a team and co-operating rather than competing with each other?

- Why do we never seem to get much done in meetings?
- What should I do when there are nasty scenes?
- How can I set up an appraisal scheme?
- How can I persuade them to do things when they seem reluctant?

Not an exhaustive list, but one which gives a taste of just some of the concerns busy managers have.

The Big Question

Perhaps the question which came through repeatedly, not using these words necessarily, was the most critical one:

- How can I be a truly great boss?

That essentially is what this book is about. It confronts major issues for busy managers and gives straightforward, no-nonsense guidance on what to do and how to do it.

All the questions above are answered and many more. If a conscious effort is made to apply the lessons in this book, we believe you will be a better and successful boss, and, let's face it, that can only be good for you, your organisation and the people who have to work for you.

Our Book Is Different

There are countless books on the management shelves, many claiming to transform you into a management Superman. So what is different about this book?

The first and most important thing is that we don't write off the cuff. We don't make things up simply because we like the sound of them. Admittedly, it is good to read about the charismatic stars of management, their wonderful experiences and their intuitive beliefs. But that is what they are – intuitive. They are not proven. What works for Joseph Bloggs Jr as chief executive of Megamotors Incorporated may not work for you as manager of a handful of staff and a budget a one-year-old could count on an abacus.

The point we are making is that relying on sermons from superstars about what you should do and shouldn't do is not a sound basis for improving yourself.

That is where we come in. We don't make things up as we go along. We delve into the management literature (and there is plenty of it) and we pull together what researchers and experts have to say. Often they agree, sometimes they don't. At least, what we have to tell you is based on the experiences of many, many people, and not just one.

Of course, our own experience comes into the picture. It is inevitable that we draw on what has happened to us as managers, and we have beliefs about what works and what doesn't. We can honestly say, however, that our practice has improved, not by reading purely inspirational books, but by basing our actions on solid evidence.

We have said it before and we'll say it again: there is nothing so practical as good theory – as the little boy here discovered.

> An elderly gentleman found a little boy sitting on the pavement crying. "What's the matter, son? Have you hurt yourself?"
> "Worse than that," sobbed the boy. "Mum has lost her book on child raising, and now she's using her own judgement!"

So it is important for all concerned to base our actions on sound principles and not simply do things intuitively.

Another way we have tried to be different is to adopt a light, easy to read, sometimes humorous approach. Again, there are books around which can be described as the 'pop' of the management literature. Often, however, they are no more than the meanderings of someone who thinks he is successful and believes everyone else should do precisely what he does.

Light-hearted and, at the same time, serious. To make the lessons stick, we have also drawn out the key learning points from the chapter topics and arranged them so they are easily understandable in the form of brief summaries.

Think ... and Then Do

This may suggest we are handing you management on a plate. Realistically, we know you can't become an accomplished manager in one minute, one week or one year. You can, however, make a real impact on your management performance by thinking about the lessons in this book and then having a go at putting them into practice.

This is important. Management does not improve by simply reading books. No doubt you have read the celebrated work *In Search of Excellence* by Peters and Waterman. It does nothing for you or your organisation, though, until you apply the lessons and principles.

The way forward with this book, then, is to read a chapter, refresh your memory at the end of it by looking at the key points, and then to THINK about how you can put some of the material into practice.

The Questions We Tackle

We have not included everything. We have tried instead to tackle the topics that some authors avoid like the plague, but which appear to cause managers a great deal of concern. Even as early as the second chapter, for example, we try to answer the central question of what makes a good manager. Not an easy task, but one that must be tackled anyway. If we don't have any idea of what a good manager is, or are not able to describe it in fairly concrete terms, how can we know what we should be working to improve?

Most of the chapters look at what the manager can *do* in order to improve his skills, make things better for the organisation, or improve conditions for employees.

In reality, all these go hand in hand. For example, if you learn how to be skilful in setting up a motivating work environment, your organisation enjoys the benefits of motivated and committed people who work harder. Your staff also enjoy their jobs more.

Similarly, if you learn when it is right to involve your staff in making decisions, your organisation gets better quality decisions, and your staff get a kick out of being in on the things that count.

In short, these are the concerns we look at:

1. What are the things I do that could make me a bad manager?
2. What is a good manager?
3. How can I help my staff get better at their jobs?
4. What does this word 'empowerment' mean and what can it do for me?
5. How can I become an effective leader?
6. How can I motivate my staff?
7. How do I know when to involve my staff in decisions?
8. How do I delegate when they don't seem interested?
9. How do I build high-performing work teams?
10. What is the right mix of people to ensure a team is effective?
11. What is the best way to make appraisal an enjoyable rather than a dreaded task?
12. When I interview someone for a job, how can I ensure I get the right person?
13. What is the best way to negotiate with people?
14. How can I get my way without seeming too bossy?
15. What should be done to make meetings purposeful and productive?
16. How should I react when there is disagreement and conflict?
17. How can I make more time for myself?

18. How should I write management reports so that they get the message across?
19. How can I deal with the dreaded presentation?
20. What sort of management structure will help people work better?

With so many questions and such a thin book, it may seem like a tall order to answer them all fully. We have not gone into excessive detail, of course, but given the key points and guidelines for action. Initially you should find these quite sufficient. But when you need to know more about, say, appraisal or team-building, you can refer to our other books which give more detailed accounts of many of these topic areas.

You've Got to Think!

Some of what we have written is thought-provoking and even controversial. That is intentional. You are supposed to think. You don't have to agree with everything. At least, if you have thought about an issue, you have then made a considered choice when you decide on which course to take.

Whatever you do, keep your mind open and avoid jumping to conclusions. This is important, as Anthony de Mello's story below shows:

> The storekeeper heard his sales assistant say to a customer, "No, we haven't had any for weeks and I doubt if we'll get any soon."
> The storekeeper rushed over to the customer as she was leaving and said, "I'm sorry, Madam, he is wrong. We'll definitely have some soon. In fact, we placed an order yesterday."
> When she had left, he said to the assistant, "Never – I repeat – *never* say we don't have something. Say we've ordered it and it will be arriving soon. Besides, what was it she wanted?"
> "Rain," answered the assistant.

We wish you a pleasant and stimulating read and, more importantly, success as you work towards becoming a 'fabulous' manager.

CHAPTER 1

What We Can Learn From Bad Managers

This chapter is about bad management. Not the most conventional way of starting a book on how to become an excellent manager, true. But you have to break down the bad to leave room for the good. If there are barriers, they have to be removed for the better practices to get in.

Also, this short journey into the realm of unfortunate practice provides an opportunity to reflect; to think about the things you do that are not helpful and productive. Like the sign on the church: "You are not too bad to come in and not too good to stay out!" Perhaps that's what we should put at the beginning of this chapter. Every manager can learn something from those who are less than perfect.

> The man was in the post office mailing a new Bible to his friend for Christmas.
> "Does the package contain anything breakable?" asked the clerk.
> "Only the Ten Commandments," replied the man.

There are no commandments as such in management, but if there were, some of the following characters we describe would not only break them – they would smash them!

We came across these examples when we were writing our earlier books. We are not talking about you – of course not! But a bit of soul searching convinced us we had been less than perfect as managers ourselves, and it did us no harm to try on the cap: if it fits, wear it.

That is the starting point – actually knowing you are not doing things right. If you have reached that stage, you're doing well.

Many of the managers we saw, however, hadn't got that far. They thought what they were doing was absolutely right. Regrettably, what some of these characters were getting up to seemed perfectly designed to destroy human relationships and prevent people from doing their best for the organisation.

The 'We Have Always Done It This Way' Manager

> The car cut across from the right lane to make a left turn and collided with another car.
> "Why no signal?" asked the correct driver.
> "Well, I always turn here!" answered the dangerous one.

He was not the only one set in his own ways. Indeed, the manager we found the most frustrating was the one who would simply refuse to let go. We called him the 'We have always done it this way' boss, because that is what he forever seemed to be saying or implying. There was only one way of doing things, and that was his way.

Like most of us, you will probably have been involved in some quality improvement movement or other, a notable one being the Total Quality Management (TQM) approach. A key feature of TQM is that

Not interested. We've always done it this way.

there are some sparkling ideas out there somewhere and if you can harness people's creativity effectively, you can do many things better.

Our traditionalist friend wasn't having any of this nonsense. Why? Because he just wouldn't accept that deficiencies existed in the internal workings of the organisation itself.

True, there are some who will listen when you tell them that they are not dealing with customers right or that there are more efficient ways of getting deliveries out. But they develop hearing difficulties when you talk about improving internal coordination and the way people relate to one another. What they fail to understand is that what goes on inside has a critical effect on the organisation's business.

We asked one 'We have always done it this way' boss why he had the most complex and time-consuming stock control system for stationery. The answer? Of course: "We have always . . ."

This phenomenon is not confined to bosses. A secretary told us: "We have never dealt with these forms", and sure enough her boss confirmed: "We have always sent people to the office at the far end of the building to collect forms".

Such managers are not necessarily resistant to change. It seems to be more a case of insular thinking. They just will not seriously question why things are being done in a particular way.

One of the stumbling blocks, of course, is the organisational culture: the beliefs and assumptions about the way things are done. Some cultures support keeping things the way they have always been.

You can get away with cultures like these in organisations that don't have to change very much. But what about those organisations that are subject to the vagaries of the fast-changing environment? If they are unable to adapt and respond, they simply die. And one of the reasons they may fail to change their systems and practices is that their cultures hold them back. Under these conditions, it is not surprising that their managers say, "We have always done it this way".

Indeed, we have just read an excellent book by Michael Fullan who argues that conditions, more often than not, favour keeping things as they are. People who like to take risks are not encouraged. That makes it difficult when you want to change things.

These systems, procedures, processes and attitudes become set in concrete only if you let them. In truth, we often make excuses in order to stay inert. We blame the organisation, the system, our colleagues, even our customers.

The fact is, we have to change ourselves if we want things to happen. We either tolerate dependency – waiting for others to tell us what to do – or we indulge in a bit of entrepreneurial spirit and get on with things ourselves.

How can I start changing things?

What can you or the organisation do about it? One useful strategy is to have someone senior who plays 'devil's advocate' all the time. It is his job to go round asking awkward questions and challenging established practices.

He asks why there are forms to be filled in; why another department has to be informed; whether there could be a short cut to a decision, and so on. He has to be pretty senior, of course, because he is undoubtedly going to get up some people's noses.

In meetings, he tries to undermine every argument and find the flaws. And our experience is that there are plenty of flaws to find! They are worth rooting out because they make the organisation inefficient and in some cases spread discontent and unhappiness.

If you have influence over organisation policy, we suggest that the expression "We have always done it this way" and similar statements, such as "This is the way things are done", should be removed from the organisational vocabulary and replaced without delay by "If there is a better way of doing it, it will be changed". You are the one who can insist on a new language, the language of optimism and opportunity.

Of course, that needs a fundamental change in attitude, showing that the organisation is effectiveness-driven rather than governed by the power of precedent and tradition. Just because it has always been done one way does not mean it is right. The practice may in reality be costing the organisation money, and that should make a few decision makers sit up and think.

What are the implications for you as a manager? One thing for sure, you have to be pretty open. You have to open your own mind to the impact of new ideas and you have to engender a spirit of openness amongst your colleagues.

That is why those organisations that positively reward employees who come up with winning ideas are reaping the benefits. People can direct their energies into the right channels for the organisation's benefit, and that should make everyone happy.

Contrast that with the organisation that discourages people's bright ideas and punishes them if they dare challenge anything. It makes you shudder!

The 'Wisdom in High Places Only' Manager

We identified another type of manager, the 'Wisdom can only exist at the top' boss. He believes wisdom is directly proportional to the location in the hierarchy. Ideas can only be good or listened to if they come from the top. Such misplaced loyalty is touching, or, rather, pathetic.

A phenomenon we have found amongst some middle managers is the quaint belief that ideas MUST be good if they stem from above. Believe it or not, top managers have just as many crackpot ideas as anyone else.

The late Anthony de Mello tells the story of the doctor observing the lifeless figure on the bed:

> "I'm afraid your husband has departed from this life."
> Whereupon there was a muted protest from the bed: "No, I'm still alive."
> "Shut up!" said the wife. "The doctor obviously knows better than you!"

Fortunately, many organisations are dispensing with the 'ideas from the top, work from the bottom' philosophy and opening up the forum for discussion. Everyone's ideas can then be listened to.

The 'It Can't Be Done Here' Manager

Another manager we encountered is the 'It can't be done here' boss. He himself may have been indoctrinated to believe that bit of fiction. More likely, though, is that others tell him not to do anything that might upset the apple cart. Consequently, he must avoid doing anything that could change things.

He has usually developed a refined vocabulary for putting people off. "We've tried it before", and "I'd love to be able to do that, but . . .". Also, "They won't like it" is often a grossly inaccurate account of the truth. "It wouldn't go down well in this place" is another way of saying there is no culture of change.

Culture is pretty powerful. It is also people who form it. And it is people who can change it. Cultural excuses often form a convenient defence mechanism against disturbing the equilibrium. The fact is: almost anything can be done, so long as there is the will to do it. And which is more important – letting the culture dictate the way things are done, or moving down the road towards organisational success?

The 'That's a Great Idea' Manager

One manager is perhaps governed more by inactivity than tradition. We call him the 'That's a great idea' boss. Working for him is like living on a roller coaster. He encourages staff to come up with ideas and suggestions, and tells them how grateful he is for contributions, but, like the previous characters, will produce an array of excuses showing why they can't be taken on board.

There is always something in the rules and regulations, some financial constraint, or some opposition from senior management that he cites as an insurmountable obstacle. This manager is a fine example of how to de-motivate workers.

You may well argue that constraints do exist. Of course they do. Money is not in limitless supply and we don't always enjoy the utmost enthusiasm for our ideas from the executive suite.

Enthusiasm, therefore, must be tempered by the reality of the situation. Real constraints must be spelt out beforehand. Is there any point in people beavering away at ideas and work improvements if there is absolutely no chance of acceptance?

The 'Me First' Manager

You certainly can't accuse the 'Me first' boss of suffering from inertia. He is intensely busy – pursuing his own personal agenda, so much so that he has little time for his employees' concerns, which he sees as trivial.

Things are important only if they relate to his personal advancement. Because some bigwig from head office is coming, he will have everyone jumping to attention to create an impression, and will have no regard for the inconvenience to his staff.

This individual can't see further than the end of his nose. The effective managers we have encountered recognise that their advancement is tied in closely with the satisfaction of their workers. If employees are not happy and motivated, they don't perform well. It doesn't mean the manager has to hold their hands all the time, but it does mean there has to be a genuine care and concern, an attitude of "We're in this together" rather than "Me first".

The 'Zookeeper' Manager

There is a widely held view that if you feed employees bananas, they will perform like monkeys. What we call the 'Zookeeper' boss believes this. Give them more money and they will inevitably do a good job. That sounds like the height of optimism!

There are many chequebook-waving football club managers who have discovered that simply dishing out the financial goodies does not guarantee results. Reason? People are not performing monkeys.

We are not against rewards, but to use them as bargaining strategies is misguided. If every time you want something done you have to give rewards, don't be surprised to see people clinging to the cage bars waiting to be fed.

We claim to treat people as mature and responsible individuals, yet many of our actions suggest we are more like zoo attendants than real motivators.

It all stems from a lack of understanding about how people become turned on. A few extra dollars, pounds or yen don't necessarily affect performance and certainly don't light the fire in people's hearts. If we want jobs done better, we have to think more seriously about what truly motivates our staff.

The 'Spy' Manager

The most invidious practice we observed was carried out by the 'Spy' boss, but fortunately there weren't many of them.

There was one manager of a large group of professionals who instructed her clerical staff to take up inconspicuous observation positions to identify latecomers and then to report back to her. Instead of raising the matter with the employees concerned, she would keep a secret file based on the reports from her spy network. This information would then be used at appraisal time.

We find it amazing that a boss like this actually believed she could work *with* her colleagues. With her espionage network, she was promoting an organisation rife with suspicion and distrust. And who wants to work in that sort of environment?

If you want a healthy climate with lots of commitment from your workers, secret discussions, files and documents are out. People need to know precisely where they stand with you.

If you don't like something, say so. True, difficult and sometimes unpleasant issues will surface, but you have to convince your staff that there is real openness. Ask yourself, can they be entirely honest with you without fear?

The 'Anointed' Manager

It seems unfair including what we call the 'Anointed' boss in this chapter, because he may be poor at the job through no fault of his own. How does he end up in the hot seat? Because he is a good surveyor, an orderly administrator, or the longest serving employee in the department. Get the picture?

know we cause more than one or two upsets when we say s are upside down. Just think: you want a manager, someone ision and a strong sense of direction; someone who can motivate nsure high quality performance. So who do you choose? The most skilled engineer, the financial wizard, the nuclear physics expert, the oldest guy around? If you do, don't be surprised if you don't get the management expertise.

If you really want a manager or leader, that is what you have to look for. It makes sense. Why, then, do organisations often appoint the wrong people? Answer? Probably "We have always done it this way"!

Don't get us wrong on this. We are not saying that people with technical expertise should not occupy the manager's chair. Many do a great job. What we are saying is that you should not assume that being good at one thing necessarily makes him good at something else. A good salesman may not make the best sales manager. A brilliant teacher may be hopeless as school head. And the outstanding surgeon may be a lousy hospital administrator. So don't jump to the wrong conclusions.

Finally . . .

These are just a few of the labels we have given to managers who are less than effective in their practices. This may all sound pessimistic, but we can learn from these examples. If we can see bits of ourselves there, we are half way to solving the problem.

The next step is to do something about it. In many situations, though, there is no breaking down of barriers unless the will exists, and sometimes a sledgehammer is more appropriate than a nail file.

In organisations that have to do things and respond to new demands, such practices as we have described can prove a barrier to progress. We really do have to get rid of the mentality that it must be good because it has always been done this way in the past. Or, because someone tells you it can't be done here, that it is really true.

This may mean radical changes in attitude and practices in order to clear the path for development. If you can shake off these shackles, you and your staff will enjoy the fruits of success.

How to Avoid Being a Poor Boss

♦ Say to your staff: "If there is a better way of doing anything here, let's find it and get it going without delay."
♦ Let employees know that their ideas are valued and that wisdom exists throughout the organisation, not just at the top.

- Say regularly to people: "It *can* be done here if we are willing to find a way". Bear in mind that while some managers are telling everyone something is impossible, others are actually doing it.
- If you say to someone "That's a great idea", then mean it and do something about it.
- Of course you have personal ambitions. But put the work and your employees first, and you'll become respected by all.
- Don't think that dishing out money will solve performance problems. Think carefully about how your employees are motivated in the long term, not just over the next few days.
- Be open with your staff. If you are unhappy, say so. Don't spy on them, test them and talk about them behind their backs. No one wants to work in a suspicious organisation.
- If you influence the selection of managers, go for those who have the ability or potential to manage or lead. Don't assume that technical prowess automatically guarantees excellence in management.

CHAPTER 2

What Makes You a Good Manager?

For some, being a manager is a thankless task. Like the mayor of this small town:

> Residents were asked by a reporter what they thought of their mayor.
> "A liar and a cheat."
> "A pompous ass."
> "A megalomaniac."
> "A clown."
> "Totally corrupt."
> These were just some of their responses. The reporter then asked the mayor about his salary.
> "I don't get a salary," answered the mayor. "I do this for the honour!"

Well, you don't do your job for the honour necessarily. Nevertheless, it is a difficult task and one you have decided you want to do well.

We have given you some ideas on how to avoid being a rotten boss. Even if you follow the advice, however, that doesn't make you a good one. But it's a start. Now, we need to know what makes a good manager so that you have something to work towards.

A Simple Question

One thing that most of us in the academic world hate is a simple question. Why? Because it is usually the most difficult to answer. Two cases spring to mind.

One guy had been doing the most elaborate piece of research spanning two years and he was enthusiastically describing his findings to his wife, who then asked, "So what?" Since he hadn't thought through the real-life practical implications, he couldn't answer.

On another occasion, the speaker was explicating the wonders of some new training approach and how it could transform dead legs into gurus, when a member of the audience asked, "Yes, but does it teach them how to think?" It is amazing how quickly some presenters develop stutters!

Simple questions are even more difficult when the perpetrator demands an equally simple answer, something most of us are not very adept at providing. We have a useful tactic for dealing with these situations though: we ask more questions.

One such simple question was asked by a journalist who was interviewing us some time ago. Her question was, "What makes a good manager?" Our typical reply started off something like, "Well, it all depends on what you mean by . . ."

It All Depends . . .

If we are going to reach the truth about skilful management, as evasive as it sounds, a few retaliatory questions are in order.

In the first place, a lot depends on who is answering the question. In other words, where you stand in relation to the manager. For example, if you are his superior, and he is 'delivering the goods', you will probably say he is a good manager. Those who have to work for him may well describe him as a real @#$%*! See the problem?

We're always careful about listening to descriptions of so-called good managers, because the storytellers seldom have all the facts. Sometimes, employees tell you what a wonderful person the boss is. What they may be saying is that he leaves them alone and accepts any old rubbish. Quality doesn't count.

In our quest for some pearls of wisdom on the matter, we asked four management experts that very question. These were their responses:

1. Someone who combines technical skills with a sense of mission and clear goals.
2. Someone who gets things done.
3. Someone who is a good organiser, who thinks ahead and has planning skills.
4. Someone who knows how to relate to people and get the right things done; who knows the art of working smart; who can read the environment and is politically aware.

This confuses the issue even more. It raises the problem of the word 'good' and how it is interpreted. It is no wonder there are so many different perspectives about good management when even the experts don't agree.

It is not for us to say who is right or wrong, but you can see that three of the statements are about task planning, organisation and completion, and only one mentions the word 'people'. Can you really talk about management without mentioning people?

A Manager or a Leader?

The complications don't end there. The word 'management' is often used interchangeably with 'leadership'. Many management experts have tried to show how they are different, but without a great deal of success.

The problem with talking about good leaders is that people naturally start listing qualities. You have to be this, that and the other to be a good leader. It's the same for managers. You read in the press regularly about the qualities needed for success. You have to be tenacious, firm, sensitive, enthusiastic, visionary, intelligent, practical, conscientious, smart, and so on ad nauseam.

If these were accurate, there wouldn't be much hope for most of us. We think all this talk about qualities is mostly uninformed nonsense. There may be a few elements of truth, but managers are developed, not born, and it is vital to recognise that.

People Are Important

Earlier, we mentioned 'people'. For us, that is the essence of management. You can call someone a production manager, a services manager, a sales manager, a department manager, and so on. But unless he has to manage people, he is not a manager.

That, for us, is at the core of management. We are working alongside members of the human race, people who think, have feelings and opinions, expectations and aspirations. A manager, therefore, who simply 'gets things done' may be missing the key ingredient – the need to get people to turn out quality work.

Two Major Considerations

So, in deciding who is a good manager, there seems to be two major considerations. They are both equally important. First, a job has to be done: in other words, the manager has to achieve something, otherwise he fails. Second, he has to get it done through other people: he has to ensure quality work and a high level of satisfaction.

Simple. You do that already. Or do you? Our experience is that the 'people' bit is paid lip service to, but not always practised well.

If we look at management closely, we find that human influence is at the root. Difficulties occur because of people, and people are needed to solve them. This convinces us that the good manager, first and foremost, knows how to work effectively with and through people.

What Makes a Good Manager?

You have probably gathered we have been avoiding answering the simple question: What is a good manager? OK, here goes.

In general terms, our definition is one who gets tasks done well by working effectively with his people. But we have to go a step further than this.

The good manager recognises what are the right things to do (in connection with the task) and that not every situation is the same. Tasks are different – some are fairly straightforward; others are complicated. And people are different – for example, managing a group of highly qualified professionals is entirely different (not more important necessarily) from supervising machine operators.

So in terms of your relationship with your staff, your behaviour as a manager may have to change according to the situation. There are times when you have to be fairly directive, and others when it is more appropriate to be open and sharing.

The good manager knows that people are the organisation's most important asset. That means you have to hold a deep belief in development – if you develop your people, you develop the organisation's work.

The good manager empowers his people, giving them the opportunity to create, contribute and commit themselves to the work. You must therefore really value your workers and their efforts, and let them know you value them.

What Are the Right Things?

What does 'doing the right things' mean? The good manager has to read the environment and to pick up the right signals. This means you have to choose the right tasks. You must learn to recognise what is important and what is not.

The good manager concentrates on the 'key result' areas, those things that yield the maximum returns for his organisation. You musn't concern yourself with the trifling things and waste your time doing pointless little administrative chores like counting money and reading junk mail. Some bosses seem to spend more time on dreaming up silly controls and penalties like forms for this, that and the other, than concentrating on the things that matter.

We heard of one school principal who must have spent her holidays thinking up ways to antagonise her staff with petty rules and regulations; one was to ban Walkmans from the staff room. What a nonsense that is. The good manager is definitely not a 'nit picker'. Attention to detail in the things that count, yes. But not wasting time on things that don't affect results.

Striking a Balance

In short, we feel the good manager knows how to strike a balance. You must understand why you are in your exalted position – to achieve things and to do them well. You must also recognise that the only way to secure long-run achievement is to work effectively through people. You therefore understand you are not dealing with machines, but people with needs and feelings, and you behave accordingly.

The good manager is also a 'doer'. You don't blame the system, the organisation and anyone else you can think of for not being able to do things. This suggests you have to be an implementer; that your involvement extends beyond direction setting.

> A centipede saw the owl about the pain in its legs.
> "You have too many legs," said the owl. "If you were a frog with just two legs, you would have a mere fraction of the pain."
> "You're right," agreed the centipede. "Show me how to become a frog."
> "Don't bother me with implementation," chastised the owl. "I only make the policy in this place."

Of course, you too may be involved in policy formation, but as a manager, you must ensure things actually happen. This may mean you have to take risks in order to get things done, knowing you are doing them for the organisation's good. A bit different from the guy who sits there telling you his hands are tied. And how often have you heard that before?

Can You Be Good at Everything?

We may be expecting a bit much of people if we want the ideal manager: we can try of course. Our experience suggests that managers are unlikely to be outstanding at everything. So what is the solution?

I think the new boss is great!

Many organisations are now moving towards 'team' management. They have one chief who is very good at getting tasks done and at driving people to productivity, and another chief who is good on the human relations side and who concentrates on keeping employees happy and motivated.

It can work well. But if you have people at the top who are all the same, say, very much task-centred, you may be inviting failure.

Finally . . .

Management is many things, but centres around people and achievement. Sometimes people don't want to do the 'right' things. This is not an easy tension to reconcile.

The manager, however, who defines his 'key result' areas and can get the best out of the workforce, but leave them satisfied, motivated and proud to be a part of the success, is a manager truly worthy of the description 'good'. But then again, that depends on what you mean by 'good'!

How to Become a Good Manager

♦ Be flexible in your behaviour. Sometimes you need to be open and sharing; at other times, you may need to dish out orders.

♦ Treat the development of your employees as a prime task. That way, they can get better at their jobs.

♦ Give them real power to create things and to contribute. And then watch their commitment grow.

♦ Do the important things, those tasks that matter when it comes to organisational success. And do them well.

♦ Don't say "It would be difficult to do this" or "I don't think they will let me." Get them done. Know when you can take risks.

CHAPTER 3

The Manager As Developer

Improving Your Workers

It's better to help others get on than to tell them where to get off.

Brian Loton, retired CEO of BHP, Australia's largest company, recently commented that "wealth is created, not bestowed". Discussing what he believed would influence management success in the 1990s, he noted that national wealth no longer comes from natural resources but is increasingly dependent on what people know and can do.

Indeed, there appears to be an increasing recognition across the world that people are the key to productivity and success.

Why all this talk about the importance of human resources? The answer is clear. We have to concentrate on getting the best out of people if we want our organisation to:

♦ be competitive in the booming global marketplace;
♦ keep pace with rapid technological change;
♦ satisfy the needs and expectations of an increasingly enlightened workforce;
♦ follow the international trend towards decentralisation;
♦ adapt quickly and efficiently to changing and unpredictable demands and aim for continued improvement.

'Effective use of human resources', 'people management', 'human resource development' – the management press bombards us with such expressions, but what does it all mean?

Most managers will nod their heads in agreement when you talk about the importance of the workforce, optimising people's contributions to the organisation, and things like 'empowerment'. Unfortunately, much of it is just rhetoric, and no more.

Take the issue of productivity. Many managers will interpret this as getting more work out of people. Perhaps they will force them to work more hours or speed up their operations. But if you are taking the human resource question seriously, productivity efforts have to be accompanied by commensurate efforts in meeting the needs of the workforce. The satisfaction of people with their working lives has to be considered alongside organisational improvements.

A Satisfied Workforce

Satisfaction does not simply mean giving people bags of gold and subsidised lunches. It means enabling them to get a real kick out of their jobs. How does that happen? Mainly through getting better at the job and feeling the improvement.

Anyone who has played a sport will tell you how enthusiasm increases as the skill level improves. A child learning a musical instrument gains more enjoyment and satisfaction as he develops the skill to make a worthwhile contribution to the orchestra. In both these cases, development is an ongoing process. Yet, what we see in many organisations is an isolated intervention. Simply sending people on the occasional course, or listening to someone rattle on at a seminar all afternoon, to be honest, does very little for development. What is needed is a long-term commitment to development and growth.

This commitment must be reflected in the expansion of managers' roles as 'people developers'. There are three areas which require conscious attention:

♦ Self-development
♦ Individual employee development
♦ Team development

Self-development

Ask any manager about how his job has changed, and he will tell you it has become more complicated and carries more responsibilities than ever. We live in a changing world. Our organisations have to survive in changing conditions. When you go through the checkout at the supermarket nowadays, look at how your purchases are registered. Imagine how a retailer using an old-fashioned mechanical cash register would cope with a queue twelve deep.

It is not only technology that is changing. People within organisations have different aspirations, demands and expectations. In some cases, they are crying out for greater levels of participation in decision making. The effective manager, the one who can face up to all this, is the one who continues to learn and grow; who increases his skill and makes an effort to develop himself.

Individual Employee Development

A trend which is becoming increasingly evident is that of employee empowerment. The manager's job is being transformed from one of directing daily activities to that of enabling self-direction and motivation.

If you are going to operate like this, however, you have to believe in your workers, and believe that they really want to improve

I wonder how the boss manages to get them to sign up for his training courses?

themselves. This sort of attitude is more likely to lead to richer productivity and increased satisfaction for everyone.

You have to see the improvement of your workers as being the same as improving your organisation. It doesn't make sense to treat attendance at courses as perks to be dished out as little rewards once a year. Any improvement opportunity is a benefit to the workplace.

Talking about training courses, we need to dispel the myth that employee development is all about escaping from company premises to be indoctrinated by some guru at the ubiquitous course or workshop. That is not right. Development opportunities exist in many of the activities that employees face daily. It can be fostered through employee participation in making decisions, setting targets and planning. It can also take place through appraisal and supervision.

Team Development

Many problems need the brainpower of more than one person. A collective approach to complex problem solving has been shown to increase effectiveness. The manager's job then becomes one of team builder and developer; a leader who can mould individual talents, strengths and aspirations together into a productive unit.

Team development is something that has to be handled skilfully. Teams that achieve stunning outcomes don't just spring up by chance. They have to be cared for and developed, and this takes time.

Training or Development?

What does the future hold for you as a manager? Does it mean dragging your employees along with you, or is it about developing strength, skill, stamina and motivation to give them the self-will to succeed?

It is true that some companies have installed wide-ranging development programmes successfully, but many have failed, because their programmes are narrowly focused, shabbily planned and largely unsystematic.

Before you say your organisation is fine because it allocates a large training budget, don't fall into the trap of seeing training and development as precisely the same thing. If you buy in a new software package, you need to train staff how to use it. Once they can press the right buttons on the keyboard, the need for training is ended.

Development, on the other hand, is much wider. Abilities are developed in a more general way so that people can use their skills and knowledge across a range of situations. Development, for example, may be about creativity, teamwork, problem solving and flexibility. In short, workers who can develop such skills become more self-reliant and self-directed.

That is a very persuasive argument for development. Many companies, however, concern themselves only with training. Why? Because training is short term, whereas development needs a bit of long range vision. Unfortunately, many managers haven't got that and can see only as far as the ends of their noses.

The message here is that development takes time and patience:

> The great golfer Jack Nicklaus asked baseball pro Henry Aaron what sort of golfer he was. Aaron answered, "It took me seventeen years to get three thousand hits in baseball. I did it in one afternoon on the golf course!"

What attitude do you have towards your worker who wants to better himself, but the improvement may not be related to the job? Do you believe in the value of such personal development? We know of one large public sector employer who refuses permission for employees to undertake degree studies, even at the individuals' own expense and entirely in their own time, if those studies are not directly related to the job. What an iniquitous restriction! What right has any employer to deny an individual intellectual growth? Do such employers really believe they can have motivated employees when they refuse to acknowledge the need for personal development and achievement?

So, try to see development in a broad way. Not simply about pulling the right levers and connecting the correct wires. Look on development as learning and growth, not simply instruction. As Winston Churchill once quipped, "I cannot stand being taught – but I enjoy learning."

What Does Development Mean in Practice?

OK, so what can you do in practical terms? You can start off by thinking in terms of formal and informal development opportunities. Some of the formal methods you can use are apprenticeships, observations, demonstrations and practice, and attending outside courses. While these are very much tied to training, they can also include development components.

Informal methods could include encouraging junior employees (maybe managers) to spend some time with experienced colleagues. You can also promote job swapping, taking part in professional association activities, and encouraging employees to meet together in teams to discuss improvements in the workplace.

More important than the methods you use are the conditions you set up. These are essential for a 'development-rich' environment:

1. Create an atmosphere that stimulates interest in getting better and that promotes the desire to become more competent and creative.
2. Encourage voluntary participation in interest groups, informal discussions, and decision making.
3. Make your reward system support risk taking and innovation.
4. Take the time to identify organisational *and* personal needs, and design development programmes around those needs.

Finally . . .

Development, for us, is one of the key words for managers. It is nothing new, but it needs some new thinking. We are doing too much at present, unwittingly maybe, to impede development.

If we are to be truly successful in the future, we may need an urgent and radical rethink about the way we approach the development of our most precious resources. And if we do that, our people may give us the magic key to higher levels of productivity and prosperity.

How to Approach the Issue of Development

♦ Enable your staff to get a kick out of their jobs and to feel responsible for their improvement.
♦ Make your own improvement as a manager a priority.
♦ Forget about just sending people on courses. Treat development as something that can be achieved in many of the normal day-to-day activities at work.
♦ Develop your role as a team builder. Teams are becoming more and more important in organisations.
♦ Think about development rather than just training. Consider the development of abilities that can be used flexibly; and the building of creativity and teamwork.
♦ Show support for personal development that might not necessarily be linked to the job.
♦ Let your staff become really involved in decisions that count.
♦ Support risk taking and dreaming up new ideas.
♦ Consider both your organisation's needs and those of the individual. See if you can match the two. That's a winning formula.

CHAPTER 4

Sharing Power With Your People

"Look! Who's the boss around here? You're paid to do as you're told, so don't come here with fancy ideas!"

Ring any bells? Most people will recognise such an admonishment. How would you react? Well, there is little you can say when someone tells you he is more important than you. Some people simply switch off, others get angry, some keep their ideas to themselves, or in extreme cases they look for greener pastures.

Nobody enjoys working in a situation where he is treated like a mindless robot. And that goes for bosses too, if only they would realise it. If they squash initiative and alienate people, they only manage to make more work for themselves.

The Traditional Picture

Traditional views of leadership pictured the big boss (usually male) sitting on top of a hierarchical pyramid, dispensing wisdom, knowledge and decisions like a doctor writing prescriptions. Such approaches have treated organisations as sterile entities which need to be controlled and driven, without much consideration of the human dynamics of people working together.

Researchers have studied processes, profits, inputs, outputs, structures and anything else they can think of. What seems to be missing, however, is a greater understanding of the human element. Organisations are not machines. They are priceless collections of individuals with their own skills, strengths, values, assumptions and beliefs.

Empowerment

Fortunately, not all bosses treat their employees like pawns. There are actually some who can identify leadership potential in their charges and try to prise it out. In short, they aim to empower their staff to become leaders in their own right.

On the other hand, there are those who break out in an anxious sweat when you suggest they should let anyone have a say in anything. They would probably prefer to tear out the page in the dictionary that contains the word 'empowerment'.

It is certainly one of the buzzwords of the 1990s. Before going on, let's take a brief look at what it means, or, first, what it *doesn't* mean.

What empowerment is not

Empowerment does not mean giving away the farm. It is not about paying everybody the same or calling 532 workers together every time a decision needs to be made about the colour of the toilet paper. It is

I am empowering you, Jones, to decide on the colour of the toilet paper ... Don't forget to obtain my permission first!

simply allowing people to exercise leadership in areas where they have expertise, interest and commitment.

Many people confuse the term empowerment with other ideas. Others take it and build their own mischievous meanings. For example, *pretending* to share power with employees runs a serious risk of back-firing and turning them off for good. Below are how a number of different managers have approached and communicated the meaning of empowerment:

- ◆ I'm going to empower you by letting you be totally in charge of ordering and distributing toilet cleaning supplies and stationery for secretaries, and the allocation of seat covers for company cars.
- ◆ I'm going to empower you by giving you much more responsibility in your job. This shows I trust you and, by golly, you had better work hard and not let me down.
- ◆ I'm going to empower you by presenting you with my own and the senior management's ideas and letting you believe they are your own.
- ◆ I'm going to empower you by making you come to every meeting on every issue and forcing you to participate in every discussion at any time I see fit. And don't let me hear any complaints that you cannot participate or I'll make you discuss that as well.
- ◆ I'm going to empower you to contribute to the organisation by giving you a bonus every time I like one of your suggestions. I hope to like at least seven suggestions each quarter, but may not like some as much as others, in which case, I will reward on the basis of whether I like the idea a lot, a bit, a reasonable amount, a little . . .

Empowerment? No! In fact, most of the above approaches have used the wrong word. Some are closer to bribery, coercion, bullying and even dishonesty than to any form of shared decision making.

Real empowerment aims to encourage people to think for themselves, to approach problems in different ways, to use their skills and abilities, and to feel good about themselves and their commitment. It is about sharing important decisions with workers and providing genuine opportunities for them to shape and mould organisational goals. Rather different from ordering toilet cleaning supplies!

The Leader's Role in Empowerment

With empowerment, the leader's job becomes one of leading employees to lead themselves. Once the ground rules are set, workers don't need to be told what to do every minute of the day. As Abraham Lincoln once said, "You cannot help men permanently by doing for them what they could and should do for themselves."

Of course, you can't transform an organisation overnight, but there are several steps you can take towards building a culture of cooperation and respect.

Understanding and Valuing

Before attempting to move towards empowerment, the leader needs an in-depth understanding of the culture of the organisation. This will have a major impact on what he can and can't do. For example, if the culture has always been based on individual competition, or 'dog-eat-dog', introducing empowerment may need to be approached differently from that of a company that has learnt how to work co-operatively.

Would-be sharers in any organisation need to communicate clearly that they value the ideas and development of their staff. It is not enough to state this in a company policy document or even to paint it in huge red letters on the roof of head office. It must be backed up by actions. Moves towards empowerment will be treated with derision if you run a meeting like Florence, Customer Services Manager in a large public sector organisation:

> Florence had called a meeting to brainstorm new ideas for streamlining customer inquiries. She had called all her staff together and made a big deal of telling them how much she valued their opinions and would be guided by their input. The staff were quite excited by this and spent several long hours working out ideas and suggestions to present at the next meeting.
>
> Within ten minutes of the start, however, they felt as though Florence had thrown six buckets of icy water over them. Her responses to the initial ideas:
>
> "Get real, Bob. Did the fairies help you with one?"
>
> "Sure, Sue, and then when you've done that, see if Santa can drop me off a Merc!"
>
> "You missed your calling, Haji. You should have been a stand-up comedian!"
>
> After half an hour the ideas stopped completely, so Florence presented her plan, and the rest of the group supported it without a murmur.

So, moves towards empowerment must be seen as real by everyone. They have to know that their ideas are valued. Florence clearly showed them that their contributions were worthless.

Giving Direction

At the base of any effort towards empowerment is a shared understanding of where the organisation is going – what it expects to achieve. Successful leaders have a clear vision of where they want to take their companies, departments or units. To get employees to share this vision, the leader must communicate its thrust clearly and ensure everybody understands.

The empowering leader makes it quite clear what is valued and is not afraid to express it, even though it may mean touching a raw nerve or two occasionally.

A clear outline vision is one thing: the details are something else. Paths towards the vision should not be 'carved in stone'. People need to be free to work within fluid organisational boundaries.

Working Together

Sharing power and decision making requires the leader to build a culture that encourages and values collaboration rather than competition. It is important to grasp that requirement. There is little point in making noises about working together if structures are in place that reward only individuals and ignore team or group efforts. Imagine if individual members of a soccer team were rewarded for scoring goals or the number of times they touched the ball during a match. They would be fighting each other! It sounds ridiculous, but that is what happens in organisations. People talk about working together, yet the rewards support individualism.

Tony: Sorry, Geoff, but I must have the ball off you. One more goal and I'm on an extra 200 bucks.

Geoff: No you don't. The longer I hang on to the ball, the more the boss reckons I'm controlling the game. That's worth 50.

Giving the Power to Act

The leader must give people the power to work towards organisational goals. In terms of real empowerment, this involves letting them decide the 'how'. Without this sort of discretion, you may as well simply tell people what to do.

Take, for example, the case of a company whose main goal is to double its sales of printers within the next year. The goal is clear. One manager communicates this to his staff and gives them a detailed point by point account of how it should be achieved. No questions. Get on and do it. Another boss also communicates the goal, but asks his staff to develop strategies for increasing sales. Which manager is more likely to get innovative ideas? Which boss is likely to have the more committed sales staff? Which boss has truly empowered his workers?

Assigning Those Tasks

Empowering leaders are well clued up on delegation. They think about the assignment of responsibilities carefully. They don't simply flog the willing horse, but give responsibility to those who may have new ideas or who can develop professionally from being involved.

Many managers make the mistake of assigning all major responsibilities to one or two people they believe they can trust.

> "Anne, before you go home, could you pull out the last two quarters' results, extract the Eastern Sector details, put them into report form with recommendations for improvement, then make twenty-five copies and leave them on my desk. I know you'll do a good job, as always."

Anne, of course, is probably sick of this already. She either puts up with it or burns out and takes a job as a gardener. While this is going on, the rest of the staff are being sent a very clear message that they are not trusted, cannot learn and are not valued. For all the contributions they are allowed to make, they may as well be working as gardeners now!

Responsibility, as we shall see when we look at motivating your staff, is a strategy the best bosses use with skill. But make it positive:

> The boss wanted someone who could be responsible. "You obviously want me," said Bill. "Every time something goes wrong here, I'm told I'm responsible!"

Making That Input Real

Empowering leaders share important decisions with their colleagues. By important, we mean those decisions that count: in other words, they have the potential to affect the organisation's productivity or quality output. They are not merely throw-away decisions that mean little to anybody. By all means, let people have something to say about the canteen menu – it's good to have some opinions on the quality of the roast duck. But what about giving them a real say in streamlining production or marketing new lines? These are the things that truly matter.

Remember the example earlier of the boss who thought empowerment was about dishing out trivial tasks. His idea of empowerment certainly did not involve staff in any important decisions, unless of course the type of cleaning agents used in the bathrooms was vital to organisational productivity.

Surrendering Some Control

Providing workers with real involvement in decision making has a number of implications for leaders. First, it forces them to share some of their power and give up some control. We know only too well that this is not easy, especially for those who have become accustomed to their godlike status. But managers wanting to share their leadership genuinely must give employees the power to pursue goals. Without the sharing of power, the very term empowerment loses all meaning.

Relinquishing some control means that there must be trust and a belief in people's ability to achieve. Empowerment is not one-sided. Employees who are encouraged to share leadership must also be willing to share responsibility and accountability with the manager.

Taking Risks

Such a process necessitates a degree of risk. One company, anxious to improve its products, put up a large sign for employees:

To err is human; to forgive divine – neither of which is the policy of this company.

But if empowerment is to lead to organisational success, mistakes and failures must be viewed positively. They must be seen as opportunities to learn.

When Jim was promoted, he asked the elderly Mr Low, whom he would be replacing, for his advice.
"Make the right decisions," said the old man.
"How do I do that?" asked Jim.
"Experience," answered Mr Low.
"But how do I get experience?"
"Make the wrong decisions."

Indeed, both managers and their employees must be willing to learn from things that go wrong. They must take risks and share both the fruits of success and also the disappointments of failure.

This can be quite a shift for many in the organisation. Traditionally, failures have been greeted with rebukes, punishments and even sackings – not things that people want a share of.

Finally . . .

Empowerment is not a Marxist plot. It is a very positive statement that reflects the value an organisation puts in its workers. It is about giving staff a real share in meaningful organisational decisions and providing them with the opportunity to influence overall goals. It is about encouraging the sort of collaboration that yields worthwhile ideas and high performance. In short, it is about sharing leadership within the organisation.

How to Empower Your Staff

- ◆ Before moving full-on towards empowerment, make sure you understand the culture of the organisation.
- ◆ Clarify your own values and express these to staff.
- ◆ Back up your words with actions.
- ◆ Engender collaboration and cooperation rather than competition.
- ◆ Clearly communicate your vision and values.
- ◆ Give staff the power to work towards organisational goals.
- ◆ Assign tasks carefully, and try to empower everybody.
- ◆ Don't 'flog the willing horse'.
- ◆ Ensure involvement is real. Value staff input and ideas.
- ◆ Empowerment involves taking risks. Success and failure become common property.

CHAPTER 5

Leadership

It's More Than Who You Are

Our trusted friend and mentor once gave us this advice: "Write about almost anything you like, delegation, teambuilding, resource management, brain surgery, nuclear physics if you must, but never write about that elusive subject which would trap even the most seasoned academic: leadership."

We are either bad listeners or fools, but it would have been unforgivable to omit leadership from any discussion of 'The Fabulous Manager'. Leadership is certainly one of the most written about topics in management. It is also one of the most confusing, carrying such descriptions as transactional, transformational, charismatic, strategic, educative, value-added, participative, empowering – to name only a few. The first thing a leader needs is a dictionary!

When we were writing for a prominent business newspaper in Southeast Asia, we managed to steer clear of the topic for a while, but later felt impelled to respond to much of the incoherent rhetoric that seems to appear with monotonous regularity. It seemed to us that virtually anything could be said by anybody about the nature of leadership. Much of it people seemed to swallow. As a result, several totally unfounded notions about leadership have become widely accepted. In this chapter, we shall try to challenge some of these beliefs, but, at the same time, provide clear guidance on what you can do to move closer to becoming a 'fabulous' leader.

It's something to do with a new participative leadership style he read about.

Easy Images

The image of leadership that springs to most people's minds is one of someone up front, pulling the troops (willing or unwilling) along. In other words, the boss is not boss unless he is flexing his muscles.

> Some zoo visitors were surprised to see a cage labelled 'Coexistence' containing a lion and some lambs. "It works well," explained the zookeeper. "We just add a few lambs from time to time!"

Employees, too, are often treated like dispensable commodities. But is this what leadership is really about? Is it simply about drilling obedient compliance into people?

We would argue that it is not. All too often, leadership is equated with leading machines rather than human beings with feelings, aspirations and reasons for complying. That poses a problem for those so-called leaders who conveniently choose to ignore the complex sets of needs that people have.

> Boss: Fred, have workers 362B, 198R, and 921P get themselves in a truck and off to the mine to sort the problem out. Tell them they'll be away for three days.
>
> Fred: But Burt was given tomorrow off to get married.
>
> Boss: We're not a social agency. If he wants to keep his job, he'll go. Another thing: tell 362B this is his last chance to do a job right.
>
> Fred: OK, I'll tell Burt the bad news. By the way, thanks for the last chance!

He Was Born Like That

Whenever you ask managers what leadership means to them (we do it frequently) you invariably end up with a long list of attributes, all very persuasive. But can aspiring managers really acquire twenty or thirty spurious qualities?

What never ceases to amaze us is the belief that you have to meet all the listed requirements to be an excellent leader. Most of these tend to be qualities. If you really do have to possess them all, we give up!

People expect an enormous amount from leaders, true. But can aspiring managers really acquire so many qualities? And what are these qualities anyway?

The trouble is that even the experts could never agree on the characteristics of an ideal leader. All sorts of worthy attributes were listed: such things as intelligence, dependability, tenacity, charisma, social inclination and many more. Despite all this, no one has ever really been able to say convincingly what a good leader needs, or should be like.

He Has More Paper

Apart from qualities, we often get hung up on certificates and diplomas. As if the number of letters someone has after his name can really predict success as a leader! We're not saying being a bright spark doesn't help, but giving a leadership position to someone just because he can wallpaper the entire executive suite with his 'pieces of paper' may be a mistake. Paper qualifications will no more make a leader than a smart haircut will.

You Are What You Are – Aren't You?

Another problem with looking at leadership from a 'qualities' angle is that it assumes that good leaders must be selected but cannot be developed. If organisations base their career structures on this premise, they offer little hope for those who want to improve their status through hard work and learning. In other words, they believe leaders are born, not made. The well-known management writer John Adair highlights the silliness of this argument in telling the story about the senior manager who wrote on a junior's report: "Smith is not a born leader, yet."

There are plenty of successful leaders around who could hardly have been born with leadership spoons in their mouths. They were never school prefects nor rugby team captains. So that tends to destroy the myth about some people having it and some not.

In fact, much of what we, as management authors, write is about development. We believe strongly in people's capacity and need to develop, for both their own satisfaction and the good of the organisation. Leaders are no exception. Indeed, the need for leadership development is arguably the most critical consideration. This seems to be particularly relevant at a time when the quality of management and leadership is being seriously questioned.

It Worked at My Place – How About Yours?

There is another major problem with looking at leadership character-istics simplistically. They don't account for the different contexts in which leadership is practised.

We all know that situations can be vastly different. The people being led may be humble operatives, or professionals with consid-erable intellect. Treat them the same? Surely not. The group may be employed on either simple, mechanistic tasks or on highly complex problems. The environment may be predictable or it may be rife with uncertainty, threat and conflict. There are so many factors which can affect the leader's situation, it is difficult to say what is appropriate behaviour across the board.

> Major Danvers was hired to lead a computer software division on the strength of his twenty-odd successful years in the army. This was his first meeting with his new troops: "Attention please. Thank you. I am honoured to lead such a successful outfit, but I intend to make a few changes round here – sharpen people up. I'm pleased to hear you work in teams – we'll call them platoons from now on. Each Division Head will report to me at 6.30 am sharp to brief me on the previous day's work. All new ideas must be personally vetted by me, and I hope we get no dissent from the ranks. Very well! Dismissed!"

Staff nearly got trampled in the rush for the employment pages of the local newspaper! Major Danvers, obviously successful in one sphere, was not sensitive to the needs of his new situation. Now, he was leading a group of highly creative people who needed a lot of autonomy in order to produce results. They may have been a bit sloppy at times, but the regimental touch would definitely impair performance.

Task-centred or People-centred?

Another school of leadership thought advances the notion that good leaders are those who can develop good relations with their staff and initiate new ways to solve problems. You may hear some advocates of this approach describing effective leaders as 'high on task, and high on people'. It simply means that they get things done well and at the same time care for the needs of people.

There is a problem with this. A tension may exist between task accomplishment and looking after the welfare of staff. There may even be different expectations. For example, middle managers, more than most, suffer from the pressures of conflicting demands. As part of management, they are responsible for productivity and task completion, but at the same time, their subordinates want their interests protected and they demand some consideration. Middle managers are often depicted as the meat in the sandwich.

This line of thinking, nevertheless, is very persuasive. It does seem that both needs have to be met. While success in achieving results is important, how it is done is of equal concern. We have seen leaders using their muscle to push things through, supervising closely, checking repeatedly, and interfering in everything. This sort of approach – get the job done and blow everyone else – is a short term one. Effective leaders in contrast have a concern for their charge's needs and lead by consent. As C.G. Jung once said: "The true leader is always led".

Changing Your Style

Another approach to leadership said that the leader should change his style according to the characteristics of his workers. Some people, for example, can set challenging goals for themselves, are willing to accept responsibility, and have lots of experience. Others are the opposite. In other words, they may be mature or immature. To complicate matters, though, some people may be mature on one type of task but immature on another type.

In short, what this approach was saying was that you have to apply the right leadership behaviour for the situation. That tends to reject the idea of one style for all occasions.

In connection with style, the question is usually asked: "Is it best to be participative or to be firm and show who is boss?". These days, most people at least pay lip service to the delights of the sharing approach.

But we must repeat that not every situation is the same. The best leaders are probably flexible, able to adapt their style to the circumstances. These may include how mature and knowledgeable the employees are: with experienced and capable people, for example, playing 'old bossy boots' may be counterproductive.

There are also other factors that might determine the right style, such as whether people can cope with uncertainty, the organisation's culture, and the time available to complete the task.

Leaders who insist on being rigid about the way they behave may actually make their workers immature by being too directive and telling them what to do and how to do it all the time. They can hardly expect their employees to develop in those conditions. The message from that is clear: If you want your employees to remain as children, lay everything on the line and don't encourage them to think.

There has been increasing agreement that leader behaviour is difficult to separate from contextual considerations. Despite this, there are skills which have to be developed before any choices can be made. This, we believe, points the way forward.

Action Leaders

We have reached the conclusion that qualities, characteristics, whims and fancies are minor considerations. Even beliefs and values may not be the keys. What is of critical importance is what the leader *does*. For example, a leader may believe in nurturing human resources, but if he treats people like dirt, his values are meaningless.

Three key factors

We see three considerations of paramount importance: the demands of the job, the groups being led, and the individuals who form those groups.

First, there is a need to achieve things; that is what you, as a leader, are there for anyway.

Second, if things are going to be done well, the group has to be cohesive. So you have to do things to make your workers gel.

Third, individual needs have to be accounted for. The needs which individuals bring to the group are very complex. If you want to influence motivation and satisfaction, you have to provide possibilities for achievement, recognition, responsibility and job interest.

If you are to be a successful leader, therefore, for our money, you have to develop skill in each of the three areas. You have to learn how to manage the task and all its associated complexities. This means much more than the day-to-day nitty gritty of getting things organised. It means sorting out your goals and priorities, and looking at what is going on around you. It also means building a vision for your organisation or unit, communicating it, and then enthusing your workers.

Difficult? We haven't finished yet! You also have to learn how to be a good people manager, so that you can get them working hard, but with real commitment. You have to show a bit of concern for their growth and development in the job, a perspective which is slightly too long for many of the myopic managers we have seen.

If you are to be competent as a leader, you need to be able to weld the diverse talents of individuals into a productive unit, like getting a football team of star individuals to play together well. If you get this right, your outfit should produce more than the sum of the individual parts. Achieving this synergy is one of the critical tasks for the skilled leader.

Getting It Together

How do these three strands fit together? If you achieve the task, the effect will be to create a sense of unity in the group and to satisfy individuals. If individuals are fully involved and motivated, they will contribute much more to the team and the team is much more likely to achieve quality results. By contrast, lack of group cohesion affects the achievement of the task and need fulfilment of individuals.

Achieving all this is not easy. But that is the point: leadership is not easy. It has to be worked at day by day. That is a message that needs to be relayed to any manager who aspires to be a leader in the true sense of the word.

Finally . . .

Leadership is receiving much attention at a time when organisations are undergoing dramatic changes. This is right, because it is critical to organisational success. Perhaps now is the time for change.

The tourist guide, showing visitors a building in the older part of the city, told them nothing had been touched or altered in 100 years. "Just like my boss," muttered one man.

Perhaps there are many of us who could echo those sentiments. But change is crucial. Modern organisations undoubtedly need leadership of quality. In an era of constant change and development, we believe there has never been a greater need for skilled and reflective leaders of people.

How to Become a More Effective Leader

♦ Think how you can improve management of tasks, like tackling problems more systematically or getting ideas from more people.

♦ Consider the needs of individuals. What do they expect from their work? Think about how you can match their personal goals with your goals. Also, consider how they are motivated.

♦ Work out strategies for getting the team to play together. Show people how their work is important and how it relates to the work of others.

♦ Think about your situation and the sort of people you have. Are they self-directed or do they expect a lot of guidance? Adapt your style to the circumstances.

♦ Try to strike a balance. Don't become so task-conscious that you ignore people's needs. At the same time, if you don't encourage quality work, people will lose their motivation.

CHAPTER 6

Motivation Means More Than Money

A manager, with renewed enthusiasm after returning from attending a three-day course on motivation, called one of his most difficult workers to his office and said, "From now on, I'm giving you the power to plan and control your own work. You can decide what resources you need and decide your own time input. That should lead to better results."

"Will I be paid more?" asked the employee.

"No, definitely not. Money is not a motivator and according to Herzberg's theory, you would get no satisfaction from a rise in pay."

"If results get better as you say, will I be paid more?"

"You obviously don't understand anything about the motivation theory," said the exasperated manager. "Now take this book home and read it. It explains all about what motivates you."

"OK, then," said the worker as he took the book. "If I read it, will I be paid more?"

We'd be fools to suggest money has no part to play in motivation, but does it really turn people on? Let's rephrase that: Does money guarantee *lasting* motivation and commitment? That, of course, puts it in a different light.

Well, if money is not the answer to the motivation problem, what is? That's precisely what we want to look at in this chapter – what you can do to get people working with a bit of fire in their hearts.

"I just can't get the beggars to work any harder. In my day it was an honest day's pay for an honest day's work. I pay them well enough but they still have lead weights in their boots. What more can I do?"

What indeed? Familiar sentiments? We seem to hear them all the time. The football club manager complains his team never performs, despite the more than generous pay. The school head bemoans the fact teachers never want to get involved in school life after the bell rings, even though they have a decent salary and a pension to look forward to. And so on.

Where these people get it wrong is in assuming that money is the be all and end all when it comes to working better and harder. We would suggest that people are looking for more out of their working lives than dollar bills dangled at the end of a piece of string.

Of course, money is important. People may be attracted to a job because of the salary, and they are certainly not going to turn up at eight on Monday morning for no reward at all. But once they are in the job, what effect does it have? Very little. And that is where motivation comes in.

If you want people to work harder or smarter, you have to start thinking about things other than cash. How can they get a kick out of their jobs? How can they do things over and above what they are paid for? How can they be encouraged to be creative and to show

It's the only way I ever seem to be able to motivate them!

infectious enthusiasm? These are the key questions.

In this chapter, we shall try to answer them and explain how you can be a manager who thinks beyond simplistic monetary reward and who builds up workers who have a desire to do well, and who want to take their performance to greater heights.

They're Not All the Same

Before we look at what might motivate your staff, let's clarify a few issues. First, motivation is not something that can be administered like a pill. This means that it is highly unlikely you can directly motivate a person sufficiently to have any real effect. Motivation must come from within a person, from his beliefs and needs.

So why you may ask, if we can't do anything about it, do we even bother discussing it? The answer is that you can do a tremendous amount to develop a work environment conducive to motivational behaviour. The way people approach their work can be significantly influenced by the conditions and culture you establish.

Second, people are motivated in different ways, depending on their needs, preferences and values. You will be singularly unsuccessful, therefore, if you treat everyone as if they were the same. Although that may sound like common sense, how often have you heard managers say "If I do this, will it motivate my staff"? They talk about people collectively as if everyone behaves and responds in precisely the same way. For our money, nothing could be further from the truth.

You only have to look round and you can see some people going crazy for power. Others couldn't care two hoots about being in control. They may be turned on by having pleasant relationships with others.

People are different and need to be treated differently. The manager who knows something about motivation talks about individuals and the subtle strategies he employs that reflect his understanding of why individuals behave the way they do.

The message from all this is that you have to know your workers. If you know them well enough, you should be able to answer at least some of the following questions:

- ◆ What do they expect to derive from their work?
- ◆ What is important to them?
- ◆ Do they expect constant recognition?
- ◆ Are they hoping to gain or extend skills?
- ◆ Are they looking for friendship and acceptance?
- ◆ Are they trying to prove something?

Whatever distinctive emphases there might be amongst individuals, you have to at least try to tie their personal goals to what you are trying to do in the organisation.

One writer on motivation claims this is the most important consideration of the lot. If people see that their personal desires are linked to organisational objectives, they will work hard, they will be satisfied with their jobs, and they will be loyal and committed to success. From this angle, getting to know individual drives is a must.

Despite the problem of individual uniqueness, you can still do things across the board to heighten the chances of motivation taking a hold. We call it 'setting the climate'. It doesn't mean you will guarantee motivation, but it does mean you will be giving it the best chance of succeeding. If you don't promote the right conditions, motivated workers may remain people you read about in books.

Giving People Challenge

Providing challenge and work that has real value is a powerful motivational strategy. People want to see their jobs as personally meaningful. If they are simply given easy, routine tasks, they will soon become dissatisfied. Imagine Churchill briefing his generals while sucking on a huge Havana:

> "Montgomery, you organise the Home Guard to rake sand on the beaches. Mountbatten, you take the Fifth Battalion and take care of the lawn on the hills. Brown, for heaven's sake, get those trenches tidied up!"

Not the best example of meaningful work!

There are several ways of providing challenge. One is to involve staff purposefully in decisions about the job. And we mean real decisions, not the peripheral things that are worth nothing. Other ways in which you can challenge your workers include giving them more responsibility for how they do their jobs, showing them that what they do is truly valued, showing that their work is important to the unit or organisation, and providing feedback on the performance of their tasks.

Making Their Input Meaningful

People obviously feel more valuable if they are purposefully involved in real decisions. It usually leads to greater commitment. To illustrate this, a story is told about a famous Formula Series driver.

One rainy Tuesday, the team's boss enthusiastically informed the driver that the new car had just arrived, and asked him to put it on the track and push it to the limit. To the boss's surprise, the driver replied, "You expect me to take that 375-horsepower beast out on a wet track when I know nothing about it and had nothing to do with its development? You know full well I need to be in on these things from the start. You want it taken to the limit. Well, take it out yourself."

People also feel better about themselves if their ideas are sought, accepted and implemented. This certainly encourages them to commit that extra effort.

Involvement can be encouraged in a number of ways. You can seek opinions and ideas, and you can consult your staff about important matters. But be warned. Involvement must be real. If it's seen as a sham, you won't get much cooperation in future.

I Did It!

You know what the feeling of doing something well is like. You may have made a picture frame or painted the house. When you can look at a completed job with satisfaction, it feels good.

Of course, we are turned on by different things. Some of us may get exhilarated by completing a marathon, whereas others may feel a sense of achievement if they can scale the front door steps without dropping from exhaustion!

Achieving something important can be a very powerful source of motivation. While it lasts, it is good. Unfortunately, this sense of accomplishment doesn't go on for ever. In fact, the more achievement we experience, the sooner it wears off. For this reason, opportunities must be provided for people to experience achievement and success regularly.

The message for bosses is clear. You sometimes have to provide the opportunity for individuals to experience a big dollop of achievement, but probably more important, you also have to give them the chance to enjoy smaller accomplishments regularly. These are the things that promote motivation.

What is it like to have a group of achievers working for you? High powered achievers like lots of responsibility, they set themselves tricky targets, and they become preoccupied with the job or whatever they are expected to do. Isn't it worth taking achievement seriously?

I Can Do That

Most individuals thrive on responsibility. As we said earlier, they are more likely to be committed to the task if it is shared with them. This means giving out pretty big doses of responsibility. Of course, doing that involves a bit of risk and a lot of trust. But if you don't do it, how are you going to ensure staff are capable of taking on increased responsibility in the future?

We are not saying you should make the risks dangerous ones. For example, it would be foolish to gamble with company profits or to risk your market standing. Look at it this way: what may be a minor responsibility to you may be highly significant to one of your staff. It's a question of perception. Part of the skill in dishing out responsibility is being able to strike this balance.

Probably the key advantage of responsibility is that it is both a powerful and ongoing motivator. It is also a way of showing recognition of an individual's ability and competence.

Since we are now on the subject of recognition, a word of caution. Don't give out reinforcement and praise capriciously. If you do, and it is not deserved, it becomes something of a joke. A bit like the Honours list, actually. Few believe that recipients have genuinely earned their rewards. When it is really deserved, on the other hand, recognition can give a hefty motivational lift.

We are not suggesting you keep quiet when things are not perfect. Giving feedback is important. But it has to be sensitive. And it needs to be helpful and specific so that something can be done about it.

> At the end of the first month's orchestral practices, Julie asked the conductor how well she was doing. "Fine," said the conductor encouragingly. "You're the best of my worst three violinists!"

You also have to be careful about what you recognise and reinforce. If you want people to be sticklers for the rules and totally inflexible, then it's OK to give them a pat on the back when they give a customer a bad time because the rules don't allow something. If you want people to be helpful and encouraging, then those are the behaviours you have to commend.

Tools to Do the Job

Motivation to perform well can also be affected by the amount of support given by bosses. How can you support your workers? By making sure they have the tools to do the job: money, materials and time. Sometimes, it means providing a bit of help. At others, it involves showing some interest. Doing these things shows you care.

It makes sense to provide adequate resources for a good job. Constraints, however, sometimes seem to become more important than the quality of the job itself. Take the case of one organisation that gave its sales staff a pep talk on presenting a thoroughly professional image to customers, and then instructed them to travel to appointments by bus as a cost-saving measure!

We are not suggesting that sticking people in plush cars and setting them up in luxury will do a great deal for motivation. It won't. But if the resources to do the job are not there, it can be demotivating. Why? Because people get the message that you don't care. The work is not that important.

Alright, skimping on resources is not disastrous, but the same can't be said for personal support in the form of recognition and responsibility. If you don't pay attention to these, you can say goodbye to motivation.

Talking about support also raises the question of the work environment. Same as resources, we don't think it is a critical motivational factor, but get it wrong, and you have a whole load of dissatisfaction on your hands. We worked together in a building where the power went off every time there was a storm. Being plunged into darkness every couple of weeks stirred up the grumbling. It doesn't mean that dissatisfaction wipes out motivation, but it certainly interferes with it.

How much do you care for your staff? Are they worth a decent bit of furniture? Are they worth decorating the office for? Are their work conditions as pleasant as yours?

We think managers should be concerned when people start complaining about the work environment, because it is usually symptomatic of other problems. We have found that highly motivated staff seldom complain about these things. Of course, one of your staff may protest genuinely because the chair is falling apart, but quite often it may have something to do with a morale problem, and it is best if you take it seriously.

Growth Is Important

Staff who are given the opportunity to develop, both professionally and personally, are more likely to be motivated. By providing and encouraging a wide range of development opportunities, you show staff that you are interested in them improving themselves and that the organisation supports and values this. If they see you are willing to commit resources to their development, they may feel more positively disposed towards the company.

What Are Your Expectations?

How well people themselves expect to do, and how much the boss expects can again be powerful sources of motivation. In other words, expectations can affect people's behaviour and how well they perform. The quality and quantity of work you expect from your staff influences both their attitude and performance. Tell them you know they can do it and they'll give their guts for you. Tell them you don't have much confidence in them, and they'll prove you right!

> Bert had a fairly important task which had to be completed before the next board meeting. "This is a big one, gang, so I'm sure you, Andrew and Pete, will understand if I don't get you to do it. I think Bill had better deal with the important stuff – I know he'll do it properly. Andrew, perhaps you can look into getting three new chairs..."

Hit me again, you might say!

Of course, most managers are not quite so forthright as Bert, but the same message is often communicated. What sort of job do you think the 'rejects' would do in their other work?

Expectations, therefore, are important. You need to consider what your expectations are. What do you believe about people's capabilities? Do you see your workers as a load of dead legs, who would rather lie down and have a sleep when your back is turned than do a good job? Or do you know they are good and really want to do a top-class job?

High expectations are communicated in very subtle ways and people pick up the signals very easily. If you, as a manager, have high expectations, you stand more chance of developing a 'high performance culture' where people work to capacity.

One caution before we leave this point. It is not clever to set impossible expectations. That leads to failure. And failure is a tremendous demotivator. So don't tell your marketing manager you confidently expect him to triple profits in the next six weeks. He will either faint or scream. Be reasonable and realistic.

Finally . . .

There's no point in taking just one strategy and expecting it to transform the motivation of your workers. What you have to do is to look at the issues we have discussed and then use them in combination to create an atmosphere characterised by high expectations, achievement, trust, responsibility and development. Doing things this way increases your chances of developing a happy, productive and motivated group of workers.

Motivated people are worth having. Who are they? They are the ones who are energetic, intense and determined, and they give far more than what is considered normal. Now you can see how the workplace can be more productive if motivation takes a widespread grip.

Just one final point – you can see from the above that you have to be pretty skilful if you are to get motivation right. The occasional pep talk may be OK, but to use it as your sole source of motivation? Well . . .

The athletics coach had the lousiest track team in the South. At every meeting, they finished last. Someone eventually listened in to one of his high powered pep talks before the events. His most inspirational comment was to tell the runners "to keep turning left and hurry back!"

How to Create Conditions for a Motivated Workforce

- Make work challenging.
- Give staff the opportunity to achieve things, however small.
- Show people that their contributions are worthwhile and valued by both you and the organisation.
- Design jobs and allocate tasks that provide people with the sort of responsibility that matches their capabilities.
- Give staff considerable control over their jobs.
- Involve them in decision making.
- Encourage them to develop and to advance their present skills, knowledge and ability.
- Always provide recognition and praise, when it is deserved.
- Set high, but realistic, expectations for staff.
- Give people the support they need. Make sure they have adequate resources.

CHAPTER 7

Who Makes the Decisions Around Here?

The young hiker was exhausted after a hard day's walking and the only place he could find was a farmhouse. He knocked on the door. The farmer explained he was short of space, and the young man could either sleep with baby or in the barn. Deciding he needed a bit of peace and quiet, he chose the barn, despite the smell. The next morning, he was stirred by a beautiful, shapely young woman carrying the pails for milking.

"Good morning," she said.

"Good morning," replied the young man. "And what is your name?"

"Everyone round here calls me 'baby'," she said. "And what's your name?"

"You can call me 'idiot'!"

Not all our decisions work out as we would like. We can't get it right all the time. But at least we can give ourselves the best chance of making the right decision.

One of the most topical issues today is whether we should make decisions on our own or let others help us. That was a problem the young man didn't have to face, since there was no one else around to help him anyway.

But for managers, it is a different matter, and it is a real problem coping with often conflicting advice. Management writers tell them one moment that they should always involve their employees in decision making, and then the next they are reminded that they are the leaders and they are paid to make the decisions.

The real issue here, however, is not whether you should be a

I've called you all here to decide on the colour of my dog's new bowl.

participative manager, but when and to what degree you should share involvement. There is no situation where shared decision making is a must. How do you decide, therefore, when it is right to share decisions and when it is best to take them on your own? There are no absolutely hard and fast rules, but there are some useful hints for deciding who decides.

Are All Decisions the Same?

The answer to that is simply 'No'. There are several types of decisions, and these should determine how much you should involve your employees. We like to think of decisions as being in three broad categories:

- ♦ Everyday decisions
- ♦ Crisis decisions
- ♦ Deep decisions

Everyday Decisions

Mike: My computer is playing up. Can I use yours until they have been to fix it?

Joan: How long do you need it for?
Mike: Ten years ought to do it.
Joan: OK, Smarty, you can have it for the afternoon.

A simple everyday decision was all that was required. Joan dealt with it very quickly using common sense. The procedure was straight-forward: she simply had to give her permission. It would have been a nonsense to involve other people.

Most everyday decisions are routine, repetitive and simple. They can often be dealt with by referring to established rules, policies and procedures. Even if they are not, you probably have a good idea of what you can and cannot do, and you can deal with them almost automatically. Most everyday decisions require little creativity and rarely do other staff need to be involved.

Crisis Decisions

"Peter? Jane here. Stop everything you're doing and get on the phone to all our bookings for today. I have decided to close the sports hall immediately. Some water got through the roof last night and lifted a few of the tiles in the changing rooms. One of our customers tripped, landed on her bare *&%$ on the cleaner's trolley, which rolled through the swing doors and dumped her in the privet hedge. She is threatening to sue us for attempted murder and embarrassment. The repairers can't come for two days, so I am planning for a three-day shutdown. I'd better call the boss with the bad news."

These decisions usually require quick, precise action, and need to be made almost immediately. If Jane, as manager of the sports complex, had not reacted promptly, and if another customer had a more serious accident, her organisation might have faced some legal difficulties.

These situations usually crop up without any advance notice and demand your immediate, undivided attention. Real crisis situations allow little time for planning or involving other people, and that was certainly the case for Jane.

Deep Decisions

Anthony had worked for weeks on his strategy for improving customer relations. It was now the weekly meeting and he was ready to tell his staff what it involved. "First," he announced, "we will stay open for an extra two hours per day. Second, we will personally visit customers to discuss business at any time from 7 am to 10 pm if they need us. Third, I would like you to invite important customers to your homes and entertain them so that you get to know them better. Fourth . . ."

Anthony didn't get any further. The angry mumblings told him that his edicts were not being received with consummate enthusiasm! He wondered what the problem was. His workteam was usually cooperative. Just last week he had told them he was going to re-allocate parking spaces. They hadn't complained then. What was the problem this time?

Anthony made the mistake of confusing an everyday decision with a *deep* decision. Just because no one bothered too much about the odd change of parking space didn't mean he could turn their lives upside down.

Deep decisions are certainly not straightforward and they require concentrated reflection, discussion and planning. They usually involve all sorts of complications – economic, social and personal. These are the types of decisions that involve the most debate, disagreement and, often, conflict. They also involve much time. Anthony had not even bothered to get everyone together and ask them what they thought about his radical ideas.

Deep decisions are very important. They are the ones that make a real difference to the company, like setting the direction and keeping the organisation on top of the competitive pile. They are also the decisions which involve the generation of complex and creative insights in often poorly understood situations. They usually affect many people. If you want the best decision in such situations, you will probably need to involve others.

So the first step in deciding who should decide is to look at the type of decision: is it *everyday*, *crisis* or *deep*? The first two types may need to be dealt with speedily, so it doesn't make sense to involve others. Deep decisions, on the other hand, are complicated, and you are a brave person indeed if you think you can always find the best outcome on your own.

Now let's look at these important decisions and try to work out who you should involve and to what extent you should involve them. There are several things you need to think of.

Know-how

If you face complex decisions like Anthony's, you probably need to involve people who have the know-how or expertise to contribute. Such people can spot the constraints and consequences. As Werner Heisenberg observed rather wisely: "An expert is someone who knows some of the worst mistakes that can be made in his subject, and how to avoid them".

Expert involvement will usually produce higher quality decisions – and that is important. But involve only those who have a real contribution to make. People's time is too valuable to waste unnecessarily. For example, if you are searching for ways of improving your computer system, there is little point in involving someone who curses the screen every day at four o'clock because he can't understand why the soap opera won't come on!

Can They Live With It?

Another consideration is whether a decision has a better chance of working if it is accepted by the employees who have to live with it and make it work. It is true that people are more likely to be committed to a decision if they are involved in making it, especially if it is going to affect either their private or working lives.

Failing to involve people who have a personal stake in a decision can have bad effects, both in terms of getting things done and for morale. On the other hand, forcing people to become involved in decisions which mean little or nothing to them is a waste of time. Let's return to Anthony and see how he could have saved his bacon if he had thought about these two things.

Anthony decided to extend company hours so that the reception facility would be more easily available to customers for a longer period of time. He did this with good intention, because he was thinking about the convenience to customers.

But he forgot about his staff. They obviously had a stake in the decision, and it was no surprise they weren't ecstatically happy about his ideas. Even one of his most valued staff had this to say: "If we obey those commands, we shan't even have private lives anymore. Besides, I can tell you what my wife will say if I tell her I am taking customers home every night – and it isn't very polite!"

The staff were the ones who would have to implement the decision and make drastic changes in their lifestyles. He didn't bargain for the fact that they would be resistant.

What Anthony should have done was to find out first about their willingness to cooperate in such a scheme. If he had, he would certainly have got a very clear answer. Additionally, he could have used their expert know-how on how important the revised arrangements would be to customers, and he might have discovered that his plans were not quite so universally popular with customers after all.

How Good Is It?

It is fairly clear that deep decisions made by teams are generally of a higher quality than those made by one individual. Quality is important in deep decisions where there are ideally a wide range of alternatives. The quality of the decision comes from a team of people generating creative ideas, evaluating constraints and possible consequences, and then deciding on the best possible solution. Here, creativity is the key.

There is general agreement that, with an increasingly complex marketplace, organisations which can successfully develop and implement creative approaches to gain customer support are likely to be successful.

So, to recap, *know-how*, *acceptance* and *quality* are probably the three most important factors, but there are still a few more you need to consider: our old enemy – time; then, your own experience; and, finally, the organisation's norms.

How Long Have You Got?

Often, you would like more time to make a decision, but this is not always possible. Sometimes you will be faced with a very important decision but find it was supposed to be made yesterday. In such cases you simply do not have the time to involve other people. You've got to make the decision and face the consequences all by yourself.

Take the case of the trainee doctor who found himself alone and facing the daunting sight of a woman being carried out of a taxi and starting to give birth. His senior colleagues were tied up either in the operating theatre or on the golf course. With little experience of delivering babies, he would have liked to have taken advice from his three-handicap colleagues, but obviously didn't have time. He had to decide what to do there and then.

Hopefully, you will not be faced with too many decisions as urgent as that one, but you will often face time constraints. This can sometimes present problems, since time may be vital to gain the commitment of your staff for implementing the decision.

Don't think you can save time by making deep decisions on your own. Yes, you can save some time on the decision itself, but you will lose it all and more when you have to explain the decision, get commitment for it and then implement it. On the other hand, if you involve people, it may take considerably longer to make the decision, but less time should be taken up with implementation.

Why, in My Day . . .

Another factor to consider is your own experience of making decisions. If you are relatively new to a leadership position and are called upon to make a major decision, it makes sense to get a bit of help from those who know what they are doing.

Manager:	I've just sent a note to Mr Marchant telling him not to bother sending that consultant again. Her ideas were a bit silly, anyway. What was her name? Barbara something or other?
Supervisor:	I think it was Barbara Marchant.
Manager:	Marchant? Whoops!
Supervisor:	You did mention it was *your* decision, didn't you?

That's How We Do Things Around Here

If your organisation has always believed in involving employees in deep decisions which affect them, and you disregard this, you will become unpopular with superiors and subordinates alike. You may also end up with a low quality decision.

Conversely, if you move into an organisation which has not traditionally encouraged employee participation in decision making, you may encounter one or two problems at first. So what is normal practice may affect to some extent the approach you can take.

This doesn't mean you have to accept what you find. You can change things, but don't rush it. If people are not used to having a say, start small. Let them loose on less dangerous decisions first, and then build up to the more monumental episodes.

Finally, when thinking about who and how much to involve others in decisions you should also consider how you work best. Do you trust your workers? Do you really value their input? If you go through a cosmetic consultative process, you may be asking for trouble. Involvement is right for this day and age, but it also opens up a few things many people would rather keep concealed. So, be prepared.

Finally . . .

You should now realise that although participative decision making is valuable in many situations, in others, it can actually be counterproductive. A lot is written about shared decision making, but it is not all sweetness and light. As T.S. Elliot once wrote: "A good deal of confusion could be avoided, if we refrained from setting before the group, what can be the aim only of the individual; and before society as a whole, what can be the aim only of the group."

As a final note, some people hate making any kind of decision. The story is told of the indecisive manager who went to a psychiatrist. The latter listened at length to the patient.

"It appears to me," said the psychiatrist, "you have a serious problem with making decisions. Do you agree?"

The manager replied, "Well, yes and no."

How to Improve Your Decision Making

♦ Separate your decisions into *everyday, crisis* and *deep*.
♦ Only deep decisions generally require group involvement.
♦ Involve people in the decision if they have some expertise in the area.
♦ Involve those who have a stake in the decision.
♦ Judicious involvement leads to better quality decisions.
♦ Solo decisions take less time to make but more time to communicate and implement.
♦ Shared decisions take longer to make but less time to gain commitment and to implement.
♦ Your own experience should influence the amount of involvement you give.
♦ The way your set-up normally operates can have a real impact on the success of participative decision making. So get people used to involvement gradually.

CHAPTER 8

Delegating or Dishing Out Work?

Julian's office door was open. Sitting deep in the plush executive chair, his feet were on the desk as he carefully studied the football scores. It was 2.30 pm. How was it he managed to find time to relax at what is usually the busiest time of the day?

"I just delegate everything," Julian boasted. "It keeps the beggars busy."

It sounded simple, but Julian wasn't offering a miracle to the overburdened executive. We had a hunch, however, he would need just that – a miracle – before too long.

Julian thought he was doing the right thing. All the books told him to delegate, so he did. What he didn't realise was that he was not delegating at all.

Delegation is one of those things that every manager tries to do, but, unfortunately, few do well. For instance, some think that dumping menial chores on the less powerful is what delegation is about. Others think it means dishing out a task and then monitoring more closely than the KGB to make sure it is done properly. Let's look at a couple of examples to show how not to do it.

Tartonia Loses Her Head

It is written that the once great leader of Barsenovia, Queen Tartonia, ordered her Chamberlain to organise a grand celebration for her tenth anniversary as ruler. At every committee meeting, however, the Queen could not help herself from turning up and taking over. She constantly interjected and questioned her supposedly trusted charge on items ranging from who should attend the lavish celebratory banquet to how low commoners would be expected to bow when she graced the streets with her presence.

Before too long, the Chamberlain became sick and tired of this. In fact, he became so angry at what he saw as Tartonia's lack of trust in his ability, that he organised a separate celebration, one with a different purpose. While the celebration was still months away Tartonia's reign had well and truly ended. Because she was too engrossed in the finer details of the supposedly delegated task, she failed to spot the revolt. She also failed to keep her head!

How many managers are like that and can't restrain themselves from interfering? They would do well to heed President Roosevelt's advice: "The best executive is the one who has sense enough to pick good men to do what he wants done and then the self-restraint to keep from meddling with them while they are doing it."

The issue, however, is not that straightforward. Managers can't simply delegate and then do a disappearing act, or else the outcomes can be catastrophic. Once again, the following sad story warns us about going too far the other way.

I'm going to delegate the nuclear deterrent programme to you. Don't bother me until you've finished.

Sang Nila Loses Some Friends

Prince Sang Nila Utama delegated a most important mission to his trusted right-hand man, Icana Doit, and then let him get on with it. Several months later, the lieutenant returned and said: "Great Prince, I and my men have completed the job awarded your humble servant. We have pillaged and burnt down the fortresses of the North!"

"You idiot," cried the prince. " I told you the East. I have no enemies in the North!"

The lieutenant rubbed his beard contemplatively and then said: "You do now, Prince."

So being an abdicator, like Sang Nila, is just as ineffective as being an interfering busybody like Tartonia. Some managers think they are delegating when they are not. They are simply dishing out work and telling people what to do, without offering a single ounce of support.

Both the Queen and the Prince thought they were delegating – it's no wonder the term has become confused. What is 'proper' delegation, then? Is it easy? And how can we improve our delegation skills so we keep our heads and our allies?

What Real Delegation Is

The key to understanding successful delegation is in three words:

◆ Authority
◆ Discretion
◆ Accountability

These simple words can help you discover whether you are really delegating or not.

Let's look at the first one. If you delegate properly, you are giving part of your job to someone else. Note we said *your* job. You can't delegate someone else's work. If it is part of your job, you are therefore giving that person the authority to do it.

Authority is important, but, on its own, it is not enough. It must be accompanied by a certain amount of discretion on how the job will be done. But – and this is the difficult bit for many managers – because it is still part of your job, you are ultimately accountable. That is the harsh reality, but also the exciting opportunity, of delegation. Sang Nila gave part of his job to the lieutenant, but he still had to 'carry the can' as far as his charge's monumental blunder was concerned.

It Isn't Easy

As we have seen, successful delegation is not easy and, in our experience, many managers try to avoid it. You'll hear all sorts of reasons. You may have used some yourself: "Bill's not up to it"; "Muriel doesn't want any extra work"; or "I can do it myself a lot faster than they can".

If you say these sorts of things, consider your own values and beliefs. It is pretty well accepted in the management world now that most employees like to be challenged by high expectations. If you hold back from delegating because you are afraid they might make mistakes, or that they might do a better job than you (banish the thought!), you may be committing a serious error. You risk spreading yourself too thinly by trying to do everything, and that does no one any good.

Let's forget the excuses and look at what you can do to increase your delegation skills – not only to keep your job, but actually to make it easier.

Some Critical Questions

If you want to improve, ask yourself four important questions:

- ◆ Am I really using the abilities of my staff?
- ◆ Could someone else do the task and benefit as a result?
- ◆ Do I think I'm indispensable?
- ◆ Could someone else do this task and free me for more important things?

What were your answers? Many managers, if they are being honest, answer 'No' to the first question. Although this is a problem, at least it demonstrates a recognition that abilities are needed in the organisation.

If, however, you answered 'Yes' to the third question, you have a more serious problem. Some people call it 'megalomania'. We don't. We see it simply as misplaced optimism! Would the organisation really fall apart if you were off sick for six months? If you think of yourself as 'Supermanager' and see the whole organisation crumbling around your ears if you don't have your finger in every pie, you are probably fooling yourself and retarding organisational and personal growth.

One highly regarded manager told us she was normally quite happy being sent for trips abroad because her unit worked just as well when she wasn't there. That's the way it should be. Such modesty and realism are all too uncommon.

We are not advocating total delegation of all tasks. You have to be careful what you delegate. There are some tasks which are ready-made for delegating, but others which must remain in your court. Critical parts of your job such as direction setting, motivation, disciplining and appraisal *must* be undertaken by you. There are numerous other tasks, however, which, if delegated, can both save you time and also present valuable learning experiences for your colleagues.

Doing It Right

That last sentence gives a clue to one of the most valuable features of delegation. If it is done properly, it is closely tied to *development*. If you emphasise this focus, you will probably find that other benefits will follow. Beware, however, of thinking that delegation is as simple as calling someone in and giving him a job (remember Sang Nila). It requires skill and practice to get it right. But it is worth developing the skill, as it will almost certainly pay off in the long run.

How do we get it right? Let's re-examine Tartonia's weak attempt at delegation and see where she went wrong. We'll do this by taking her through a scheme which would at least have helped her think about delegation in a systematic way.

Think

Exercise the old grey matter. Think about the task. Don't delegate the rubbish, the jobs you don't enjoy doing. You will not be contributing to people's development and you will lose their respect.

> The newspaper's senior reporter did not gain the respect of his two juniors when he delegated the task of covering the story about the main power cable that had fallen across High Street. "We don't know if it is still live or not," he said, "so one of you should get hold of it and the other can write the story."

At least, Tartonia did not dish out a meaningless chore. She saw herself as delegating the most important task in the land. After all, it would have been unfitting for her to be seen planning her own celebrations.

Prepare

When the task to be delegated has been selected, you need to prepare for handing over to the employee. Notice we wrote 'handing', not 'throwing' or 'kicking'. In order to do this properly, you should be able to answer a number of vital questions:

- ◆ What is it expected to achieve?
- ◆ How will success be judged?
- ◆ When must it be completed?

It is useful to jot down a few notes and also to consider what resources might be needed. This information can form what is known as a *task brief*. Don't give these notes biblical authority. Remember, the person to whom you are delegating should have some say.

Tartonia prepared by . . . Well, you can be the judge. Below is the note she scribbled when preparing to hand over the task:

> "Plan the most lavish celebration that has ever been experienced in Barsenovia and have it ready by 19 June."

Adequately prepared? Hmm!

Select

When you've worked out most of the details, it's time to decide who the lucky 'volunteer' will be. Bear in mind, though, that, although Fred is trustworthy and capable, he may be the willing four-legged creature who has been flogged just once too often.

One of the real benefits of delegation is that it can be an excellent vehicle for developing staff through giving them responsibility and showing trust in their potential. It may be a mistake to assume that it has to be the one you can always trust. So ask yourself: who is ready for and could benefit from delegation? Then you can attempt to match the person and the task.

Once again, Tartonia got it wrong. She automatically selected her Chamberlain, because he was the most important person (besides the royals) in the land. She didn't consider anyone else, nor did she think about the huge responsibilities he already had.

Meet

After choosing someone, meet with him or her to discuss the job and your expectations. Use the task brief prepared earlier and talk it through, but allow the employee to decide 'how' to do it.

Give the whole task, not just bits and pieces. That way, the person can own responsibility for it. Always hand the task over face-to-face and provide any other material which may be useful.

By the end of the meeting you should both understand the details associated with task completion and have reached mutual agreement on how to proceed. The best way to do this is in the form of a contract.

Tartonia simply sent the note she had written to the Chamberlain and asked him to inform her when the meeting dates would be, as she had a 'few ideas'. You can probably imagine the Chamberlain's reaction!

Contract

The contract should confirm a number of areas:

♦ Exact nature of the task
♦ Required outcomes
♦ Performance criteria
♦ Time frame
♦ Authority and resources needed
♦ Agreed monitoring points

The fact that you should contract agreed monitoring points shows that you can't back off completely, even when you have formalised the contract.

The contract, though, was not really an issue for Tartonia. She didn't have one. As a result, she gave the Chamberlain the impression that he could proceed as he wished.

Monitor

The nurse shook the sleeping patient. "Come on, wake up."
"What's wrong?" asked the patient drowsily.
"Nothing. It's just time for your sleeping tablet."

Unnecessary interference can be a pain in the proverbial for the delegate. At the same time, you can't afford to let go completely. You need to monitor progress for the sake of yourself and the other person. There is a very fine dividing line between over-interference and abdication. Like teaching a young child to swim, you need to be around for support in the early stages, but as he gets more confident, you can stand further back and leave him to it. That needs a fair bit of skilled judgement.

As we said earlier, you remain ultimately accountable for the task, so some monitoring is always necessary. This does not mean you should take over the chair at meetings, even if you are the undisputed boss. Monitor only at agreed points and play a strong support role, one that assists and develops the employee and ensures that the task is 'on track'.

This is where Tartonia really messed it up. Sure, she wouldn't have got an A-plus for how she delegated to this point, but it was her constant interference and nitpicking that finally pushed the Chamberlain over the edge. Without realising it, she sent a very clear message to him that he was not trusted and was thought incapable of dealing with such a complex task. As we now know, she looked over his shoulder once too often.

Review

Finally, you should evaluate how well the task was done, your employee's performance, and perhaps your level of achievement as a delegator. Identify strengths and weaknesses, and use these when planning for the next task. If targets have been realistically set, it should not be a problem measuring performance.

If you follow the scheme above, evaluating the process itself should be a little easier. The hard part is reviewing your own role. Were you fair? Did the employee develop? Was it a 'real' task?

Unfortunately, Tartonia did not reach this stage. The only opportunity she had to evaluate her performance was as they pulled the hood over her head. Could she have been thinking about what might have been? One good thing came out of it: at his enthronement ceremony, the Chamberlain promised publicly he would sharpen his delegation skills at every opportunity!

Finally . . .

Unfortunately, delegation is a sadly neglected and poorly practised managerial skill. So next time you complain of being underpaid, undervalued and overworked, remember that by delegating properly, you can do something about the last one. What's more, you can also develop your staff, and if that means they are more competent and motivated, the effort must be worth it.

How to Improve Your Delegating Skill

♦ Think about the task before you delegate. Decide what will be involved.

♦ Choose the right employee: one who has the necessary skills and knowledge, or one who will benefit from completing the task.

♦ Ensure the delegate is clear about what is expected.

- Give the delegate real input on how the task should be planned, developed and implemented. Try to delegate complete tasks.
- Do not overload particular staff members.
- Delegate authority and responsibility. Trust your staff to complete the task.
- Establish time frames and deadlines for the task.
- Provide encouragement and be tolerant of mistakes – remember, people learn from mistakes.
- Monitor progression towards task completion only at agreed points.
- Carefully evaluate the outcomes, the process involved, and your performance as delegator.

CHAPTER 9

Ruining or Developing Teamwork

Take Your Choice

How to Ruin Teamwork in Thirteen Easy Lessons

There is much talk in the management press nowadays about teams: management teams, production teams, marketing teams, work improvement teams and so on. Teams, as most people know, are all about involvement. But, if you are tired of all this democratic stuff about participation and sharing, we provide some tips on how to put spokes in the wheels of teamwork:

♦ Don't bother getting all the information needed for a good decision.
♦ Don't waste time discussing other people's ideas.
♦ Accept there is only one way of doing things and everything else must be wrong.
♦ Don't let team members have differences of opinion: it will spoil the atmosphere.
♦ Don't attempt anything unfamiliar: it is best to stick with what you know.
♦ Take it as an insult if anyone dares to disagree with you.
♦ State frequently: "We have always done it this way!"
♦ Give members jobs to do based on precedent, regardless of whether those members are any good at doing them.
♦ Avoid action, otherwise people will not want to be members of the team.
♦ If things don't go well, blame other team members.

- Ignore the needs of others and consider only your own interests.
- Be as polite as possible and avoid discussing anything contentious.
- Be extremely formal and cite rules and regulations to prevent people from contributing to discussions.

Of course, we are being facetious, although it has to be said there are many who behave like that and believe that they run effective teams!

In this chapter, we want to focus on how teams can *really* work and how they can be used as a powerful source of improvement to the organisation. And that is important. They can transform the performance of your organisation. Remember in Chapter 3 we talked about one aspect of development being to develop teamwork? Now we look at why it is necessary and how to do it.

So we are going to be talking about development. But we also push the idea of openness quite frequently. These two words – development and openness – are very important to teamwork.

I'm beginning to think we should never have sent the marketing team on that Interpersonal Skills course.

Development

Take development first. Managers are indeed recognising the value of teams in developing the work of the organisation. Better decisions are made and cooperative effort generally leads to higher levels of commitment and more impressive outcomes. Development also means improvement in the working lives of employees and their relationships with fellow workers.

The benefits of people working together cooperatively apply to any type of team. But teams have to be managed skilfully if they are to produce quality results. Just putting people together does not guarantee success. Many soccer managers have discovered to their dismay that you can't simply throw a collection of individuals together, however talented, and be sure of quality results.

Sad to say, too many teams in organisations are formed just like that, and some radical rethinking may need to be done about the way they are managed and led. The success of teams has to be worked at: it won't happen by chance.

So what can we do to improve teamwork? Basically, we have to ensure that four conditions are present:

♦ Shared targets
♦ Quality relationships
♦ A sense of pulling together
♦ Balanced leadership

Shared Targets

A consultant, working with the senior management team of a small manufacturing company, interviewed members of the team individually and posed them a question which had never been addressed before. He asked them: "What do you understand to be the key purpose of this company?" One response was: "to expand distribution to other parts of the region"; another: "to add another two product lines before the end of next year"; yet another who had very strong social inclinations: "to provide jobs for this area which has low unemployment". The managing director's response was "to make as much *brass* (money) as possible!"

There wasn't exactly much cohesion there! It is difficult to see how a team can work well together if it isn't sure where it is going. Imagine a football team not sure about which goal to shoot at! A common sense of direction and purpose is essential.

So the first thing to do is to outline in the simplest terms possible the key purpose of the team's operation. It may be: "to make substantial improvements in the way customers are treated at reception", or: "to decide the level of our diversification strategy in the next three years".

Quality Relationships

If teams are going to work, relationships must be of a high quality. This is where we often run into difficulties when we conduct team development workshops. Many managers mistakenly believe that high quality interactions occur through people simply being nice to one another. True, team members have to get on well together, but just being pleasant and avoiding disagreement does little to enhance team performance.

Quality relationships are present only when people can argue without the team falling apart. They should be able to disagree without resentment setting in.

We remember one team meeting we attended in Singapore where disagreement over a policy issue was openly voiced by one member. The look of shock, it was later revealed, was because no one had shown the temerity before to present a dissenting viewpoint. It was a cultural expectation that the leader's stand would be rubber-stamped by the polite consensual nods.

Of course, we are not suggesting that people should be insensitive: on the contrary, they must be tactful and know the things to say and the things not to say. But they have to be able to express their feelings. Those who keep themselves at a 'respectable' distance from other team members are probably a hindrance to team development.

These are the ones who are often excessively formal in their communication with others:

> One member of the management committee was in hospital and being visited by another, more senior member. The latter said: "The committee wishes to express regret on your illness and hopes a full and speedy recovery will be expedited. That was passed by a majority of six to one, with one abstention."

Apart from informality, there must also be depth to discussions. Those who restrict themselves to superficialities are likely to inhibit teamwork, since relationships will tend to remain shallow and, in some cases, false.

In our work, we have come across so-called teams that have been together for years, but the relationships are so superficial, they don't even know how many children others have. Their social discussions seem to be limited to the weather, car engines and gripes about work.

Earlier, along with development, we mentioned openness. Many managers we come into contact with state that communication in the management team is completely open. We sometimes wonder, however, when we witness some poorly thought out major decisions about policy issues, whether the communication really is open or whether team members have been encouraged to keep their opinions to themselves to protect their advancement opportunities!

Pulling Together

People have to behave as a team rather than as a group of disparate individuals. They must recognise that the team is there to complete a task and it is more than an individual can manage.

> The band had just finished a rousing, if out-of-tune, rendition of a grand march. The audience applauded with polite enthusiasm. The conductor then said to his players, "Now we'll play the 'Thunder and Lightning Polka'."
> "Oh, no," moaned the trombonist, "I've just finished playing that!"

Team cohesion suggests players should be playing the same tune. At the same time, it does not mean they should all be playing the same instrument.

Individual differences

Team members each bring with them their individual differences in terms of personality make-up and a set of skills and experiences. The respective contributions, therefore, have to be coordinated.

Let's return briefly to the football pitch. Each player has a part to play in the drama. Some players are goal scorers, others are goal preventers, and some are adept at transferring the ball from defence to attack. Some are creative and some are fierce tacklers. All these abilities have to be coordinated. Imagine what it would be like taking to the field with eleven goalkeepers!

So when you form a team, you don't want identical people. You need diversity. Look for people who can provide one piece each of the jigsaw puzzle. Then you, as leader, must take responsibility for trying to put the pieces together.

Similarly, the team members have to understand their separate efforts are part of an overall effort leading to the team's product. If they are there simply to look nice and agree with the boss, they may as well stay at home! That is why 'yes men' are the worst team members, and why any boss who selects only those who always agree with him is likely to end up with lousy decisions and poor teamwork.

Who should be on the team?

Team membership is an issue which has raised much debate. The right combination of members can ensure that pulling together is effective. Some people have clear roles in terms of their expertise or experience. Obviously, if you have got a team together to work out a proposal for funding a development project, it makes sense to have a guy who knows what bits of paraphernalia are needed and another who knows how to navigate the financial procedures.

However, if you want to be really skilful in building teams, you have to think about more than just expertise and knowledge, important as these are.

You should also consider what can be called *process roles*; in other words, how people behave to make the team work well. For example, some are clever at coming up with innovative ways of solving problems; others are good at decoding complex information and finding the flaws in plans. Some can get on with the job and produce quality work, whilst others like to poke their noses around to see what is going on elsewhere.

All these can be important at various times to the high performing team. If everyone behaves the same, things don't work as well. We'll tell you more about this aspect of teamwork in the next chapter.

What we are really saying is: make sure you get the right people on your team. That is not the same as saying pick the most skilful or knowledgeable exponents. An interesting point.

How many should be in the team?

Apart from having the right members, you need to be careful about how many you have. The best advice we can give is to keep the team small. It is so easy to feel you have to include Joe because he has always been invited along. And Harry will be offended if Joe goes, and he doesn't. And so it goes on. But before you know it, your team has become unwieldy.

It may sound a bit simplistic, but, in a good team, you want everyone involved in the action for as much of the time as possible. If you have a one hour meeting and five members, on average, they can each talk for twelve minutes. But if you have ten members, everyone's potential contribution time is cut by half.

Of course, there are times when, for one reason or another, you need a larger team. Generally, however, you should aim to keep it small, and if you want a figure, we would say between five and eight members.

Learning to live together

We believe 'pulling together' can be made easier by developing and supporting a common language and culture. In effective teams, this happens naturally to a certain extent. Your team members learn what to say, when to say it, what is the right thing to do, how to dress and so on.

The team becomes more 'we' than 'me'. But you can also play your part by encouraging people who share the team's ideals and ways of doing things. Basically, this is all about learning to live and work together.

Balanced Leadership

Successful teams, more often than not, have a leader who knows what he is doing. We don't mean a dictator – banish the thought. We mean someone who has developed the skill of bringing the team together into a coordinated unit.

Why do we call it 'balanced leadership'? Because the team leader has to do something of a balancing act. It isn't easy. He has to balance the demands of task completion, team cohesion and individual needs. In other words, he has to get the job done. But the best way to get it done is by coordinating all the talent that exists in the team. Also, he has to ensure that individuals are motivated and get a kick out of their involvement. We said it wasn't easy!

So, the successful team leader has to reconcile these demands and ensure that high quality results are achieved through cohesive team effort and through individual members feeling their contributions have been worthwhile and recognised.

Although we keep going on about the team as a unit and everyone pulling together, team members still have to be understood as individuals. Each member is motivated by different factors and comes with a different set of experiences. Some respond well to suggestions, and some disintegrate under criticism. Some thrive under pressure, whilst others prefer calmer waters. The really good team leader has to be sensitive to these differences.

Building Winning Teams

Now let's reverse some of the items of advice we gave at the beginning and see what can make teams tick. We would suggest that effective team leaders:

♦ purposefully encourage ideas from each team member, and listen and discuss them seriously;

- really seek alternative and better ways of doing things;
- actively encourage people to find the flaws in arguments. If someone exposes an important weakness in the boss's idea, the boss should think more highly of him;
- insist on people presenting different opinions;
- try out new ideas and look for creative decisions;
- try to match tasks with people's abilities, interests and wishes;
- focus on action: people actually doing things, and not just talking about them;
- make the team accept responsibility for its successes *and* failures, and learn from the latter;
- openly consider conflicting needs and demands amongst members;
- encourage team members to get to know each other at a personal level;
- become businesslike in operation, yet promote an informal style which is open and comfortable.

Finally . . .

Teams are not a management 'fad'. They have proved to be a valuable asset to those organisations that have discovered how to build them and then to look after them.

Your job is a critical one. You have to create teams from the right materials, build them and cement them, and lead them to the sorts of quality outcomes beyond the reach of mere mortal individuals. As our Japanese friends would say, you have to nurture and stroke them.

How to Build Up Really Good Teams

- Explain in the simplest terms what the team's task is.
- Encourage members to speak openly and encourage them when they disagree.
- Choose team members who are different from one another.
- Avoid 'yes men' on your team.
- Include only those who have a real contribution to make.
- Keep the team small.
- Lead the team in a balanced way: be purposeful in the task; give your team members satisfying roles; and coordinate the talents and contributions of individuals to produce a team effort.
- Focus on action: get the team *doing* things.
- Take risks: try out ideas.

CHAPTER 10

Successful Teams
Getting the Right People

One of the most important factors in team success is having the right people. Obviously, that makes sense. But who are the right people?

This is where we run into difficulties. You can put well-intentioned people together, but their achievements as a team are often nothing to write home about. They may think they are good, but that is usually because they use the wrong yardstick: equally average teams.

Such teams think that, by getting the best brains, the leading experts or the most knowledgeable exponents, they will end up with a winning outfit.

Sadly, such teams seldom produce stunning results. Some management teams, for example, with enough certificates and diplomas between them to reconstitute a tropical rainforest, can best be described as average.

True, you need people in the team who can do the job. The marketing guy, the information technology wizard, the electronics buff, may all be necessary depending on the project, but, as we hinted in the last chapter, there is something more to it than that.

We usually miss out on a vital aspect of people in teams – the *roles* that people play in terms of their behaviour.

Roles

We know it sounds a bit far-fetched, but getting the right mix of roles together really does work. Meredith Belbin discovered that in his well-known management team research in the UK. He suggested that you can sometimes transform the work of a team if you take this roles thing seriously.

Much of this is based on an acceptance that people can't be good at everything. So it is best to find out what they prefer doing and then try to use that to advantage.

The evidence so far suggests that everyone tends to prefer certain roles. They also stick with those roles naturally. Furthermore, certain combinations of these people lead to more successful teams. And that is the very reason for taking the matter seriously.

How do you start? First, you need to find out which roles people employ naturally and see how they fit into the team plan. Below, we outline very briefly the roles described by Belbin. He gave people labels to describe the ways in which they typically like to behave.

♦ The *Coordinator* is a leader, but a very pleasant one to work with. He likes to involve others and is quite systematic. He maintains an even keel under pressure and generally keeps his cool.

♦ The *Shaper* is also a leader, but not a democrat like the Coordinator. He is seen as 'bossy boots' and tends to get up people's noses. An incisive, no-nonsense man, he likes his own ideas best, and does not mind being unpopular. Blunt and impatient, he nevertheless gets things done when others are dilly-dallying.

♦ The *Plant* is the ideas man. While others are constrained by their rigid thinking, this person dreams up some weird and wonderful ways of going about things. He is the George Best of the team, the one who can add that vital spark. He is called the Plant because, if you 'plant' him in a mediocre team, he may transform its work.

♦ The *Monitor-Evaluator* is the analyst. He looks at ideas and suggestions critically and finds the flaws. He prevents the team from going ahead with plans that are ill-advised. He is a very clever person and can often find the best solution amongst alternatives.

♦ The *Implementer* is a real grafter. He looks for clearly defined goals and tangible results, and is more concerned with doing a good, thorough job than with clever ideas.

♦ The *Team Worker* is the counsellor, the one who shows concern for people's feelings. Everyone likes him because he hates friction and tries to get people working harmoniously. He also helps his more reticent colleagues.

♦ The *Resource Investigator* likes to explore ideas outside the team. He makes useful contacts and knows what others are doing. He gets bored with the humdrum of everyday life and can be impulsive, but he is good at exploring new possibilities.

- The *Completer* is the 'nagger', the one who makes sure jobs are finished on time and done well. He can be quite irritating, but he breathes urgency and stops his team colleagues from becoming careless, over-confident or lazy.
- The *Specialist* is the one with technical expertise. He is slightly different from the others, because his personal make-up doesn't affect his membership. He may be a temporary member for as long as his specialist knowledge is needed.

If you had your colleagues in mind as you read through those descriptions, you could probably spot most of them there. However, you may have put a few of them in more than one category. That is quite normal. People sometimes do play more than one role.

You have now got an idea of what we mean by roles. In the same way we don't want people with identical skills in the team, we also don't want everyone behaving the same way. Imagine a team of 'shapers'! Everyone would be getting on one another's nerves. That takes us on to the problem of teams that are unbalanced. They have just a few roles and others are missing altogether.

Unbalanced Teams

If you think about it carefully, there seem to be many teams around in our organisations that comprise virtually nothing but Implementers. Why is this? Quite simply because they are solid and reliable, loyal company men and women. They then find themselves in important teams. They are also (and this is very important) the least likely to answer the leader back or challenge ideas.

Good for the leader if you always want your own way. But good for the team? No! Teams that are dominated by such people have a great weakness. They make do with mediocre solutions to problems because no one wants to create 'aggro'. Teams, though, need people who will test out solutions, who will find the flaws and speak up.

We like the story of the French poodle meeting the Russian wolfhound in Paris in the 1970s.

> "Russia is wonderful," said the wolfhound. "I get sumptuous food and live in luxury."
> "Why do you come to Paris then?" asked the poodle.
> "Because," the wolfhound leaned over and whispered, "sometimes, I like to bark!"

How many of us work in organisations where the mildest whimper is frowned upon? You simply can't have that state of affairs in teams.

The thing I like about this team, gentlemen, is its diversity.

The Monitor-Evaluator will certainly bark. To maintain a successful team, therefore, we must have someone with a few megacycles of brainpower, who will knock ideas back if they don't add up. He will certainly ensure high quality decisions. So it makes sense to have a bright character in the team – he may be thought of as 'clever clogs' – someone who will stop silly, ill thought-out ideas becoming law. Having everyone agreeing politely with the chairperson is a weakness that has to be remedied.

The biggest fault we can find with teams, however, is that they generally lack that vital ingredient of creativity. How often in your teams do you have people throwing around crazy and unworkable ideas? Don't mock them. Such ideas have sometimes sparked off the most astounding and profitable inventions.

If you have someone who can add that spark, who is a natural creator, treasure him. He is a rare breed. We don't find many around in our work. You may think he is crazy. But he is also worth his weight in gold and can turn a mediocre outfit into a high performing team.

How to Create a Balanced Team

What happens if these people are not around? We can't, of course, dismantle teams, but there are two things we can do. First, we may be able to introduce a new face if the team so obviously needs an additional role. Second, we can encourage members to develop their preferred roles or even to adopt others for the good of the team.

Some employees are fairly adaptable creatures (like the Coordinator and Team Worker) and will often make a good job of an unaccustomed role. It may seem strange at first encouraging someone, say, to argue with decisions and play 'devil's advocate', but it works.

To do this, you have to know what people's preferred roles are, and one way you can do this is by discussing them at a team meeting. It's quite fascinating listening to other colleagues explain how they see your role. Good fun and also very revealing. Another way is to use a questionnaire, and you can find a useful one in our book *Making Management Work*.

You will notice that we had two leaders. The brash Shaper (there are more than a few of those about) is useful in some situations, but in the longer term, the Coordinator is more likely to win the support and commitment of team colleagues.

It is good to have a mix of roles. The Teamworker makes sure the team is a pleasant place for everyone with good relationships between individuals. The Completer too, while being a pain in the nether regions, makes sure things get done on time. But the three roles which we feel are of paramount importance are Coordinator, Monitor-Evaluator and Plant. If you have these three above all others, it can mean the difference between mediocrity and excellence.

Finally . . .

The research over the period of a decade or so into team roles is convincing. It should be taken seriously. Team management looks destined to fail unless it is taken beyond the mere selection of capable colleagues.

Understanding and developing the process roles of members will, we believe, go some considerable way to elevating the performance of teams and welding them into highly productive and successful units.

How to Get a Balanced Team

♦ Find out about the process roles your team members prefer.
♦ Encourage people to develop their preferred roles or to learn other roles.
♦ Look for a Coordinator to lead the team.
♦ Ensure you have a Monitor-Evaluator and a Plant in the team.

CHAPTER 11

Making Appraisal Worthwhile

So you have an appraisal scheme and it works very well. You have a nice chat once a year, fill in a few forms, give people a bit more money (if they are lucky), and everyone is quite happy. Really?

Be honest. How productive is your appraisal system in reality? To help you answer that question, it is worth looking intently at the questions below. If appraisal is worth its salt, you should have some pretty impressive answers to each one:

♦ How do you enable your employees to measure how well they are doing?
♦ What strategies do you use to recognise their achievements?
♦ How do you support them if they want to advance their careers?
♦ How do you identify and arrange the right development activities to support effective performance on the job?
♦ How do you encourage your employees to air problems and grievances (even about your management practices)?

Only by dealing with these issues can you get to the heart of appraisal and derive real benefits from it – benefits for you, your organisation and your employees.

Are You Really Open?

There are several words which are currently in vogue in management circles. One of them we mentioned when we looked earlier at effective

You can be entirely open with me.

teams: 'openness', although we're not too sure whether some managers have cottoned on to what it means exactly. As one executive recently told us: "I have an open-door policy; I open it once a week for five minutes!"

Nowhere, however, is the spirit of openness more defied than in some of the appraisal systems which many organisations have inflicted on their employees.

> "Well, Fred, it's annual appraisal time again. What would you like to talk to me about?"
> "Absolutely nothing!" replied Fred.
> "What do you mean?" asked the stunned manager.
> "It doesn't matter what I tell you: you still write what you want, and won't let me see it."

Fred's reaction may not have been typical, but he had a point. He worked for an organisation that had secret documents – so secret that Fred wasn't allowed to see what was written about him.

They are often euphemistically called 'confidential reports' or the like, and are certainly not 'open'. It would be difficult to convince anyone with a modicum of intellect that an organisation employing these sorts of practices is open. Actions, as we all know, speak louder than words.

Why make such a song and dance about something which is widely accepted anyway? Largely because we believe in development. And what we have read about earlier has little to do with development.

We don't believe employees can develop effectively in systems that hide things from employees. And if people don't develop, bang goes any hope of achieving sustained excellence!

Proponents of 'closed' schemes would have you believe that a friendly open discussion compensates for the minor hiccup of not seeing the eulogy which the boss has written about you.

If there is nothing to hide, why hide it? A more important issue, of course, is accountability. Some executives can be trusted to record faithfully the contents of a conversation; others can't. And when someone's career may hinge on the capricious stroke of a pen, it makes the whole thing more serious. A manager who is to have the respect and trust of his staff must be able to be open with them.

Questionable Practices

Apart from the secrecy in some organisations, other things need questioning. What do clever people do when they are not sure how to evaluate something? (It isn't a riddle.) They measure it. And if it can't be measured, they measure it anyway!

It amuses us to see managers circling numbers on rating scales, trying to assess such elusive qualities as 'integrity' and 'dependability'. We still haven't managed to fathom what seven out of ten for integrity means. Does it mean the guy spends 30 per cent of his time telling lies?

Humour apart, there are very good reasons for getting to grips with performance issues, but this can only be done effectively if there is true openness between boss and subordinate.

Should Appraisal Be Linked to Pay?

Our short answer to that is a straight 'No!'. You run into all sorts of problems if appraisal is linked to such threatening issues as promotion and pay. So if you say to an employee, "Your upgrading depends on the appraisal", forget about openness. Do you really think he is going to expose his weaknesses and discuss development needs? Under these circumstances, most of us dwell at considerable length on the things that make us wonderful, and we conveniently forget our imperfections.

Many progressive organisations throughout the world have moved away from closed appraisal systems, and no longer link the process in a threatening way with pay and incentives. They have realised that closed schemes are good at breeding fear and suspicion, and are not too bad at damaging relationships either!

Let's Look Forward

We think performance *should* be assessed. But that is only part of the story, and a small part at that. More important is that people should get better at their jobs. In other words, they need to *develop*. If they improve, then the organisation gets better.

Despite the simplicity of the logic, it seems to have eluded many organisations who go to great lengths to impede development. Everything they do – structure, systems and processes – seems to make it difficult for employees to get better at their jobs.

The balance needs redressing in favour of development, and there seems to be a good case for renaming performance appraisal 'developmental appraisal'. In the end, everyone will be happy.

How Do You Make the Most of People's Potential?

If human potential is to be maximised (and that seems the only way of moving along the path to excellence), there are certain beliefs which seem fundamental to appraisal:

♦ Everyone can improve.
♦ People need to be motivated.
♦ Employees should be considered as individuals with distinct sets of needs.
♦ Areas for development should be identified and acted on.

If we can set our sights on these beliefs, there is a good chance we can get to grips with the really important issues of development and growth.

A Partnership

Much of what we advocate implies managers and employees being open with one another. Productive organisations, after all, are those where people work together (not against each other).

The word we like is 'partnership' and this is the important concept in effective appraisal. The individual and his manager *share* the responsibility for improvement in the workplace and for future development.

With this partnership in place, discussions can be open, and there can be a high degree of trust. You can ask employees about difficulties in the job and their improvement needs, and you may even get honest replies!

You can show people what you have written about them. You can ask them about the things you do that make it more difficult for your workers to operate effectively. You can even expose yourself to criticisms your employees might have about you. That is real openness.

Seeing Appraisal As an Opportunity

When we talk about appraisal, we discuss improvement, development, building on strengths, setting targets, identifying problems, difficulties and training needs. Others talk about weaknesses, failures, promotion and pay. Can you see the difference?

We are using appraisal as an opportunity for both parties to focus on those issues that will ultimately lead to organisational improvement. Isn't that, after all, the intention of all such processes?

What we are advocating, therefore, is transforming appraisal from a word which people across the organisation treat with the enthusiasm of a visit to the dentist into an occasion they can look forward to.

Using Appraisal to Build on Strengths

Appraisal should be positive, not a fault-finding exercise. You should be trying to capitalise on people's strengths, not magnifying their weaknesses. If you do this, you can make sure that the jobs you give them match up with their strengths.

We saw the case of one manager with a highly analytical mind who had developed some very innovative schemes for his company. However, his interpersonal and communication skills were sadly lacking. The organisation gave him a job that involved dealing with the public on a regular basis. His irritability had an adverse impact on business. So, not the best example of matching talent with responsibility.

Words and Action

The partnership we talked about earlier involves keeping promises. If you say you will do something, then do it. Don't make promises you can't or are unwilling to keep.

If, for instance, you agree to look into the possibility of giving a junior manager some experience of the marketing function, then you must seriously attempt to do something for him. If a year goes by and he is still doing the same thing, you and the system lose credibility. 'Action' is the word.

How to Do It

We have given plenty of advice about the principles and approach. Now a few pointers for conducting the appraisal. If you want detailed information, you will find it in our book *Making Management Work*.

Look at the forms you use. They may be boring and require information that is useless. Try including instructions and questions like these:

◆ Outline any problems that have prevented you from doing your job well. How can you overcome them?
◆ If you were in my shoes, what changes would you make to enable yourself to work better?
◆ What training or development do you need to help you do your job even better?
◆ What do you think should be your major targets during the next period?
◆ Which responsibilities would you ideally like to take on, and which would you like to discard?
◆ How do you see your career developing and how do you think I can help you?

OK, you don't have to use this wording, but do you see the point? These sorts of questions get at the real issues. They don't harp on past failures, but look to the future, and ask how the job can be done better; how the individual can be more motivated; and how everyone can move forward.

Getting the Appraisal Interview Right

If you ask your employee to think about the questions above before you hold the interview, it should go well anyway. Nevertheless, there are several things you can do to improve the process:

◆ *Involve the employee*
Let him have a go at evaluating himself and at formulating workplans. He will then get a greater sense of ownership. Also, during the interview, let him do most of the talking. You can ask the questions.

- ◆ *Be realistic*
  Go for small scale successes rather than monumental failures. Encourage ambition, but ensure it falls within the bounds of realism.
- ◆ *Be specific*
  Don't talk in vague terms. Focus on the facts. These provide the evidence for decisions.
- ◆ *Solve problems together*
  This is the partnership bit. You have to work with each other to tackle problems that are hindering successful work outcomes.
- ◆ *Allow plenty of time*
  Appraisal interviews are serious. They have serious implications for performance and for the individual's career. If you try to polish them off in 20 minutes, you obviously don't think they are worth much.
- ◆ *Choose the right time and place*
  Hold the interview at a time when you can continue until everything has been discussed satisfactorily. The place should be pleasant and comfortable. Don't sit behind your desk. It is better if you both sit on easy chairs reasonably close to each other.

These simple guidelines will help to ensure that the interview is a productive and pleasant experience. As important as it is, it can only bear fruit if the follow-up action occurs.

Using Appraisal to Transform Performance

In emphasising the developmental side of appraisal, we are really advocating transforming performance. For us, focusing on development is the only way it can be done. If we have given the impression that we are less than enthusiastic about some of the weird and wonderful assessment mechanisms around, using such instruments as rating scales and so forth, it merely reflects our distaste for pretending that everything can be turned into numbers.

We still need to be convinced that such closed judgements do anything to convert performance into the realms of excellence. But by investing your time in your workforce, its development and its satisfaction, you can expect the sorts of achievements typical of the most highly effective managers.

Finally . . .

You will have gathered that we have recognised the need to develop a good relationship between manager and employee. We accept things can go wrong, but we hope not quite so badly as in the following story!

> A spray painter stripped naked and went on the rampage, smashing his head against the windscreens of four cars outside his work-place . . . Police said the painter was angered by his supervisor's negative appraisal of his work performance (*The Straits Times*, 9 March 1991).

How to Make Appraisal a Productive and Worthwhile Experience

- Concentrate on your employees getting better at their jobs and focus the discussion on that.
- Be open with your staff and encourage them to be open with you.
- Build on people's strengths.
- Make promises only if you are able to keep them. If you agree to take some action, then make sure it happens.
- Jointly identify training and development needs.
- Set targets together.
- Discuss the types of responsibilities which the employee would like to take on.
- Discuss how you can help the employee develop his career.
- Involve him in evaluating himself and in devising work plans.
- Solve problems and work-related difficulties together.
- Be very specific and avoid vague and meaningless expressions.
- Allow plenty of time for a serious and important discussion.

CHAPTER 12

Selecting the Right Person
The Art of Interviewing

When we watch a television personality nattering away with an eloquent politician or an effusive sports star, it looks deceptively easy. Piece of cake, in fact. When most of us interview, however, the sort of information we get usually lacks depth, and may be irrelevant, inaccurate, and sometimes untruthful.

Interviewing is most certainly not easy! But it is something managers are very much involved in. Selection interviews, appraisal interviews, informal information-gathering interviews, and, sadly, disciplinary interviews. If they are going to be of any use, managers need to become good at interviewing. Then, you can at least give yourself a sporting chance of getting it right.

What is the Purpose of Interviewing?

To give the poor guy as bad a time as possible! If you watch some interviewers in action, you could be forgiven for thinking that. The basic purpose of interviewing, however, is to see things from the other person's point of view.

This means getting the person to talk. That's the only way you can find out about the way he sees things. You don't have to shut up entirely, but the time for you to talk is when he asks you questions. That makes it a two-way process – the way it should be.

Think of the job interview – the type of interviewing most managers are involved in at some time or other. You are interviewing the guy to find out if he is right for the job. At the same time, he should be interviewing you to see whether he likes you and your set-up.

What Can You Do to Make Interviews Lousy?

If you want to make interviews a waste of time, to start off, be aggressive. Decide you can't stand the guy, and try to make the event like an interrogation. Whenever he starts talking, interrupt. Don't smile and make sure you sit on a flashy executive chair, while he sits on a knee level stool. If a few of you are interviewing, sit behind a large desk so that he feels he is facing a firing squad.

Those points should get the interview off to a pretty poor start. Now let's see how you can make it worse. You can waste time going over information, most of it useless, on the application form: "What were your grades in primary school? How many GCEs did you get?"

You can also make sure your questions are unclear or, better still, unintelligible. The beauty of this strategy is that it makes the interview even more stressful for the detainee.

Don't prepare. Ignore those who tell you as much time should be spent on preparation as the interview itself.

Talk about anything apart from the job and the candidate. Encourage him to digress so that you don't have to bother with the boring stuff related to the interview's purpose.

Change roles. If you like the sound of your own voice, why not do all the talking? At least, you will find out if the guy is a good listener.

How to Make Interviews Work Well

OK. So much for how not to do it. How can you get the best from interviews and make sure they are worth the time and effort?

The right place

Find a suitable place. If you have ever tried to hold an interview while the candidate is suffering from frostbite or heatstroke, you will know what we mean. So make sure the temperature is comfortable.

If you have watched a good film and, as it gets to the thrilling bit, the adverts come on, you will understand the frustration of interruptions. Give the orders: No telephone calls. No drop-in visitors.

You don't have to confirm your regal authority by sitting on the throne. Nor do you need a castle wall between you and the enemy. Come out from behind the desk and sit on a comfortable chair near the candidate.

Well thought out

Plan it. Plan what you are going to say at the beginning and plan your questions. Plan what you will do with the answers. Get it planned

And let me tell you, son, we believe in informality in this company.

properly, and you should have time for the really important activity: listening.

Do your homework. Look at the guy's application. If the information is written down, there is no need to go over it again during the precious interview time. Use a highlighter pen to indicate the bits you want to ask him about.

Prepare a list of topics – not too many – that you want to discuss. Tick them off when they have been covered. They should tie in with each other so that you don't break the train of thought.

Think about what is important to the job and what isn't. Are primary school grades really critical to the job of Sales Director? Forget ancient history and concentrate on the things that truly matter.

The Interview Itself

How to start the interview

If you have been to a panel interview where, when you walk in, they all have their heads buried in papers and they totally ignore you, you will know it is not the most welcoming experience. Sometimes, you haven't a clue who they are and they don't even tell you.

Don't do it like that. Stand up when the person comes into the room and greet him with a smile.

Introduce the interview briefly. Give him a map. "I am interviewing you for the job of Assistant Marketing Manager. I shall be asking you about the experience you gained in your last job, what your career intentions are, and how you see your potential contribution to this department."

Then warm him up with an easy but open question. "Tell me about the main responsibilities in your present job." Leave the difficult or controversial stuff until he feels comfortable with you.

Exercise your writing hand

Take notes – brief ones. First, that tells the candidate you are interested in what he is saying. Second, you can go back to some of the points later. That way, you don't have to interrupt him. Finally, you will be able to refer to the notes after you have interviewed other candidates.

Don't write all the time, though. Do look up and give him a few encouraging nods, smiles and utterances. If you write throughout, he may feel as if he is giving dictation!

Listen

If you want a rough guide, the candidate should do about three-quarters of the talking. Your job is then to make sure he is talking about the right things. If you ask the right questions, this should be fairly easy. More about questions later.

Show a bit of support

Don't look like a stuffed dummy. The occasional nod, smile and "I see" or "yes" work wonders. They are usually guaranteed to keep him talking. Whatever you do, don't look at your watch. He will know that you have lost interest and it can have a devastating effect. Put your watch on or near your papers so that you can check the time discreetly.

You can be even more supportive with a bit of skill. Good interviewers can summarise and paraphrase really well. "So what you are saying is that some of the technicians are disappointed with the new arrangements?" Most of us find this tricky, so it needs plenty of practice.

Finish it off well

Ask the candidate if he has any questions or remarks. He may wish to reiterate something that is important to him. Hopefully, you have done some summarising as you have gone along, and now is the chance to do a brief final summary. Try to finish on a positive note.

What Are the Most Common Interviewing Problems?

Distractions

Most of us are pretty biased. That's a fact. So long as we recognise it, we can do something about it.

Like all of us, you are probably turned off by some types of clothes or hairstyles. You may not like certain accents. You may easily lose your objectivity when you interview, say, the opposite sex or tall people. That's why you need a sort of checklist with the things you are looking for written down. Then you can check the candidate's merits against those.

Halo effect

This is where someone is good at one thing, so you assume he is good at others. For example, the person may be well dressed and able to speak very well. You may then see him as intelligent and capable of dealing with people easily. You may, of course, be quite wrong. Believe it or not, many pilots have a fear of heights. Who would assume that?

False assumptions

Beware of jumping to the wrong conclusions. If someone did not have a university education, it doesn't mean he was lacking in intellect. His parents may have been 'broke'.

How to Ask Telling Questions

The real skill of interviewing comes in asking the right questions at the right time, and then using the responses to feed into more questions. This way, you can get at the truth. There are several types of questions that can help in gathering meaningful information.

'What would you do?' questions

If you use them in the right way, these are far better than the usual rubbishy questions asked at interviews. Think of a problem the guy would face in the job. Then ask him, "What would you do?" For example, "The production department is complaining that your marketing department never gives it sufficient notice of incoming orders. What would you do?"

This can reveal a lot about the candidate's way of thinking and working. You will probably have to explore the answers with some further questions, though.

Open questions

We said earlier you need to get the person talking. Open questions do just that. They demand something more than 'yes' or 'no'.

"What views do you have about this?"
"How could you improve teamwork?"

Searching questions

You can't write searching questions out in advance, but you still need to use them if you want to delve deeper:

"Why did you decide to leave?"
"What other options were open to you?"

You can also use these questions to encourage the interviewee to keep talking:

"And following that, what happened?"
"Really?"

Using these questions enables you to go below the surface and to make wiser selection decisions. However, you should know why you are asking them. It is not clever to simply dream up searching questions.

You may often have to touch on a sensitive subject. For example, you may want to get to the bottom of why he left his last job. Your first question gets a guarded response. So you ask it again in a different way. If it is really important, you can't let the matter drop.

"What were the circumstances for your leaving the company after three months?"
"Why did they not listen to your ideas?"
"How could the company have influenced you to stay?"

The Types of Questions You Should Avoid

Closed questions – those that demand a 'yes' or 'no' answer, or some simple information – don't give you very much. Use them only if you have to.

Try to avoid leading questions. These have the answer built into the question and can sound threatening:

"You would agree with me that everyone's pay should be cut by the new manager, wouldn't you?"

Muddled questions get asked all the time. The interviewer tries to ask two or more questions at one go:

"What are your views on that and how would you deal with it, bearing in mind the salary levels which are low, aren't they?"

Of course, some single questions can be muddled because they haven't been thought out properly. Make it easy for the poor guy on the receiving end of all this. If he says he doesn't understand, he is worried he may be seen as brainless. So use short words and simple questions.

Setting Up Interviews

What is the best way to set up your interviews? There are more ways of organising them than just you interviewing an individual. Each has pros and cons.

One-to-one interview

This is a cosy arrangement and is good if you get the interviewee relaxed and talking freely. But if you don't ask the right questions, there is no one else there to help you. Also, if you are unwittingly biased about something, it may be difficult to correct.

Panel interview

This is where two or more people interview one candidate. It is fine if it comprises interviewers who have valid reasons for being there. For example, they may be technical specialists or supervisors. But where they are present for political reasons, the interviews are often poor.

If you want to use a panel, you must meet beforehand and prepare. Decide who is going to ask what, and discuss what you are looking for.

Panel interviews are pretty stressful at the best of times. Try to make them as informal as you can. Sit on easy chairs in a circle. Get your co-interviewers to adopt a friendly approach. There is little to be gained from terrorising the candidate.

Immediately after the interview, compare notes and discuss briefly. However, don't reach any firm conclusions until you have interviewed everybody. Also, be aware that your impressions of candidates will change as you get tired. If it is going to take a few hours to get through the lot, then take a few coffee breaks and have a walk around. It does wonders for your concentration.

Coordinated sets

This is a way of combining the two preceding methods. Each interviewee goes through a series of one-to-one (or small panel) interviews, maybe three or four, and each interviewer has a particular brief to follow. For example, one may ask questions about career, while another may assess managerial ability.

Like the panel interview, preparation is the key. Each interviewer has to know his brief: what he is trying to find out. After the interviews, the panel meets to put all the information together.

We like this format, although, of course, it means more people being involved. It works even better if you have two interviewers in each 'set'. That way, you help to eliminate bias, and one can act as scribe, while the other asks most of the questions.

What Should You Cover in Selection Interviews?

Four areas need to be addressed:

♦ Qualifications
♦ Work background
♦ Aspirations
♦ Non-work activities

Qualifications

No need to spend much time on this. You should find the information on the form or in the CV. As we said earlier, forget about primary school test grades and concentrate on those things that are directly relevant to the job. And don't be snobbish. Someone who slogged away to get a degree at the age of forty-five is probably just as good as some whiz kid who did it all straight after school.

Work background

The most recent job is also the most important. Find out about relevant experience. But don't fall into the trap of looking for someone who has done everything before. You should be searching for someone with the capability.

Aspirations

This is important. You are looking to the future. Is he motivated? Will he get a challenge from the job, or is it all old hat? Does the job fit in with his career plans?

Non-job activities

We think you are better off with people who know how to balance their lives. You may be tempted to hire the guy who promises you 168 hours a week on the job, but the balanced individual tends to give you more quality in the long run.

Finally . . .

Have you ever come across these situations? – ten minutes to interview someone for a senior post; half a day to interview all twenty on the shortlist, even if it kills us! "We know who we want already – if you tell us anything good about yourself, we are deaf, because the other guy will get the job!"

Can't be true? Of course they are true. They happen all the time. Just think, though, if a guy is going to be with you for the next fifteen years, you'd better get it right.

Mistakes in interviews can be expensive. It makes sense, therefore, that you think about setting up the right conditions, ask the right questions and evaluate the information carefully if you want to end up with people who are right for you and your organisation.

How to Conduct Successful Selection Interviews

- ♦ Choose a congenial setting with comfortable and informally arranged furniture, and no interruptions.
- ♦ Look through the documents and prepare the questions you need to ask.
- ♦ Set a pleasant tone at the beginning and show a friendly attitude.
- ♦ Take notes.
- ♦ Listen carefully and make supportive gestures.
- ♦ Use questions that search for the truth and delve below the surface.
- ♦ Consider and discuss aspirations more than less important issues.
- ♦ If appropriate, use coordinated sets of interviews as a way of giving the candidate 'value for money'.

CHAPTER 13

Reach Agreement and Everyone Is Happy!

Jan: Why did you negotiate so much with the poor shopkeeper? You nearly bled him dry getting the price reduced like that. Anyway, you never pay his bill.

Pete: You're right, but I didn't want the guy to lose more than necessary!

We all negotiate. In fact, we do it most of the time. Maybe it's the choice of food when we go out for a meal, selecting our annual holiday venue, or the day to day rigmarole of persuading the children to go to sleep.

Some managers are pretty clever at it. Others are not so good. To start off, it is more than simple bargaining. You have to be able to read between the lines and listen to the things people *don't* say. You have to spot the signals. In other words, you have to be something of an expert communicator.

Look at the following statements taken from negotiations. Would you have taken them at face value? In fact, they were not the end of negotiation. They were cues that discussions should continue. We have suggested some interpretations of what the person might actually have been saying:

1. I'm sorry, I would find it far too difficult to put on that number of training sessions.
   I would find it difficult but I could still do it if I got something in return.

2. I'm not willing to compromise on our design package.
   I would compromise on something else.
3. Oh no, we don't usually serve meals at that time of day.
   We don't usually do it but we could if the price or the size of order was right.
4. I could not possibly cut down my costs on materials.
   I could possibly cut my costs on labour or something else though.
5. This is not the right time to discuss your promotion.
   We can discuss it at some other time.
   This is the right time to discuss something else.

That was just to start you thinking about negotiation. There is a lot more to it than that, of course. In fact, if you are going to do it really well, it takes some time to develop the skills.

Is it worth it? The answer is a big 'yes'. The key feature of negotiation is that it is about reaching agreement. That means both you and the other guy can be happy with the outcome and, equally

Arguing? No! They agreed on everything before the meeting. They told their members, though, that they would be doing some hard bargaining.

important, you can be happy with each other. Those are two very persuasive reasons for negotiating.

Do You Always Have to Negotiate?

The answer to that question is 'no'. It depends whether you want everyone to win or just yourself. For example, you can boss the other person around (only if he is a lesser mortal than you, of course). In that case, you win, he loses.

You may also be able to consult. But getting someone's opinion doesn't mean reaching agreement. It means getting his opinion!

Or you can take the easy way out by getting someone else to solve the dispute, otherwise known as 'arbitration'. "I'll refer that to the boss." You probably still end up with a winner and a loser.

The problem with these ways is that they don't make both sides happy and they don't do a great deal for personal relationships. That is where negotiation wins hands down.

How Does Negotiation Work?

First, two people (or groups) have different views about what should be done. If they don't, there is nothing to negotiate. You can go and have a party instead.

You may want one of your employees to take on a responsibility and he doesn't want to. You want goods at a particular price, but your supplier wants to charge more. You want to go for a meal, but your spouse wants to go to the cinema. All these are situations where you can negotiate.

Second, you and the other guy exchange views. You discover where you agree and disagree, then you try to resolve the differences.

Finally, you reach agreement about how to proceed. Both of you are reasonably satisfied with the outcome. You can both be committed to the solution. This won't happen if you simply use your muscle and give him an order.

Simple as that! So negotiation is fairly easy. It just involves discussing one or two sticky issues and then shaking hands. Or does it?

It would be nice if negotiation were that easy. There would be no industrial action and we would be able to sort out the discount for our new car in minutes. But there are skills involved that require effort to develop. Let's go back and look at what's involved in some of the stages.

Different views

People have different motives or interests. These determine the way they look at things. You have to find out what they are. Don't assume you are getting the whole picture through the other person's words.

Giving each other's views

You have to go through a ritual or you get it wrong. You state what you want and then listen to what the other guy wants. Then you suggest solutions and listen to the other person's solutions. You may have to shift your position a bit if you are going to get an agreement.

So you can see from this that you have to state, listen, suggest and shift. They all have to be done well.

The 'shifting' bit can be tricky. You have to know in advance how much you can shift, and that calls for pretty careful planning. You can't negotiate properly unless you do your homework. More about that shortly.

The agreement

Getting agreement is sometimes easier said than done. You may not be able to resolve differences totally, but you can agree to accommodate them. This is still reaching agreement and represents a positive outcome.

What Do You Need to Prepare Before Negotiating?

We just said you have to do a bit of homework. First of all, you have to become clear about your ideal or *target*. It would be the perfect outcome for you. It may be to get a certain figure discount on your new car.

Your realistic expectations are probably less. So, when it comes to the encounter with the salesman (who obviously does not want to give you so much discount – if any) you will probably shift ground towards your realistic figure. The important thing, though, is that you know in advance precisely how much you are prepared to move.

The very minimum you are prepared to achieve is your *threshold limit*. Anything less than that is failure and you would not be happy with the outcome.

So, before you negotiate, prepare a little map showing your target and threshold limit. Aim for the target, but be prepared to shift towards the threshold limit if necessary.

Apart from knowing what you yourself want and your limits, you should have a good idea of the other person's view and his supporting arguments. This may involve a bit of detective work or simple guesswork.

Sometimes, you may also need some information, like facts and figures, and this has to be accurate, or you can be made to look foolish if you get it wrong.

We know it sounds a bit sneaky, but if you can get some information that the other guy wants to keep to himself, it puts you in a strong position. For example, if you know he is low on orders, it may put you in a good position when you want to negotiate price or delivery dates.

At the same time, don't try and stitch him up. We are talking about negotiation, not war! Both of you have to be happy with the outcome and you want to keep relationships healthy.

You should also work out what your strengths are and the other person's weaknesses. Then, in the negotiation, you can dwell on the strengths of your argument.

Think carefully about the carrots you can use. What is important to you but not to him? What is cheap for you but advantageous for him? For example, when you buy your new car, accessories may be important to you. These are good items to negotiate on, because the dealer can get them at cost price, so they are relatively cheap to him and far better than giving you a cash discount.

Therefore, it makes sense if you can give something that does not cost you very much, but which means a lot to the other person. And vice versa.

You must be absolutely clear about the things you can move on and those you can't. If there are certain principles at stake, like everyone has to take a share of responsibility, then those things are non-negotiable.

How Do You Start the Negotiation Off?

The first thing you do is to state your position. Tell the other person what you would like ideally. Try to set this at a realistic level. There is no point in being silly, like asking for a 300 per cent pay increase, because the other person may lose interest.

Then you listen to what the other person has to say. Listen carefully – he may say more than he intended, and give you some clues about how far you can go. At this stage, don't jump to conclusions, but listen attentively. De Mello shows the drawbacks of closing your mind's doors too early:

The drunkard staggered up to the parish priest and said, "Excuse me, Father. Could you tell me what causes arthritis?"

"I'll tell you what causes arthritis," answered the priest impatiently.

"Drinking causes arthritis. Gambling causes arthritis. Visiting prostitutes causes arthritis. Now – I'm busy – why did you ask?"

"Because it said in today's paper that's what the Pope has!"

What Next?

You now have a friendly discussion about each other's demands, outlining some of the pros and cons. Don't forget to find out about what you agree on already. No point in wasting time on those things.

Now is where your skill in language comes in. Ideally, you should be doing some 'if-ing' and 'then-ing'. "*If* you were to consider doing this, *then* I might be able to offer something more." Fairly non-committal, but that is the idea. You are testing the ground.

You have to be pretty clever at this stage. Try thinking about other things you can negotiate with. For example, you may be haggling over the price with a customer, but perhaps you could throw delivery dates into the pot as well.

Don't put all your cards on the table. Hold information and concessions in reserve to leave something to bargain with. This is part of the negotiation game. It is perfectly legitimate, because you are trying to aim for your ideal target. There is no point in starting off with aims that are too modest.

If you have done the first bit properly, you may be ready for some hard bargaining now. "Now, how does this sound to you . . .?" If you have read the situation well, you should not get an outright 'no'. You may get counter-suggestions, but that is fine. It means the negotiation is getting somewhere.

Hopefully, you end up with an agreement. You need to go over what you have agreed. Memory plays tricks. Write down the agreed points if necessary.

What Happens If You Can't Agree?

There are times when the threshold limits simply don't come anywhere near each other. It is best to agree to disagree, to go away to think about it, and then to meet again some other time. Consider it a problem you are trying to solve jointly.

And above all, stay friends with the other person. There is nothing more harmful than a breakdown in relationships.

Also, you can't move if it is a question of values. In this regard, there is a difference between firmness and intransigence. Being firm in some situations is quite reasonable. Besides, there is no point in giving in to the point where you are dissatisfied with the outcome. This leads us on to consider results of negotiations that keep everyone happy.

How to Get 'Super' Agreements

If you can ensure high benefits to both sides in the negotiation, you end up with what Dean Pruitt calls 'integrative agreements'. These are likely to last, since both you and the other guy will be extremely happy with the outcome. Here are some things you can do.

Expanding the pie

You can increase the resources. For example, two of your staff want the desk near the window. You may be able to rearrange the furniture so that both desks offer a view through the window.

Unrelated swaps

You may agree to what the other person wants in return for something which is good for you but unrelated. For example, you may agree to do some extra work in exchange for some tickets to the test match.

Logrolling

This means that you give way on your low priority items in order to get what you want on the really important things. So you may reduce your price a little in order to delay delivery, because you are inundated with orders. Delivery time is of prime importance to you; price is not so important.

Cost cutting

You get what you want and the other person's costs are minimised. You want the other person to stay very late after work to complete an important project. The cost is he will miss his evening meal. You could arrange for a nice meal to be delivered specially to his office. The cost is therefore partly offset.

Bridging

You don't get your demands, but your important interests are satisfied. You want to go for a meal. Your better half wants to go to the cinema. The question to ask is: "How can we arrange our evening so that we are able to eat and enjoy some entertainment?" It doesn't have to result in a take-away in front of the telly. Hopefully, a bit of creative thinking may yield an enterprising solution. You may have to dispense with some of your low priority wishes, though.

Some Miscellaneous (or Mischievous) Negotiation Tactics

A few supportive remarks can go a long way in pushing the other guy down the right road: "Yes, I didn't really think of that, but you have a very strong point."

Rather than reach disagreement, you can quickly put it off and say: "OK, let's come back to that later." This is playing for time.

The redirected question is a tactic which is used very adeptly by many politicians. Answering a question with a question is alright sometimes, but it can get people's backs up.

Q: Are you going to give me a pay rise?
A: How do you think your colleagues would feel if you were the only one to get a rise?

Finally . . .

Negotiation is not easy, but if you think about trying to reach a situation where both you and the other person end up reasonably happy and satisfied, you shouldn't go far wrong. Reaching agreement is the true strength of this way of resolving differences.

How to Negotiate Well

- Decide what you ideally want to achieve and the minimum you will accept.
- Find out the strengths and weaknesses of the other side's case, and get hold of relevant facts and figures.
- Do your homework thoroughly. For example, find out what means a lot to the other person.
- State your expectations clearly and then let the other person do the same.
- Listen carefully to what the other person says and try to read the clues.
- Use "What if . . . then . . ." often to test the other person's response.
- Search for agreements that make both of you very happy.
- Write down what has been agreed.
- Above all, make sure you stay on good terms. No point in falling out.

CHAPTER 14

How to Get Your Way Without Being Bossy
The Skilful Influencer

Henry was determined to persuade Victoria to marry him, but his attempts to influence her had failed miserably. He then tried his *piece de resistance* and reasoned with her that his widowed father was already ninety-five years old and was disgustingly wealthy. She asked for two weeks to think it over. After the two weeks, Henry was calling Victoria 'Mother'!

Fortunately, not all our attempts at influencing go so badly wrong, but they don't work out as planned either. Since we are influencing people most of the time, there is some sense in becoming good at it.

Is the Boss a Bully?

Some people are absolutely clueless when it comes to influencing. A senior management friend told us about one of her colleagues who did not allow talking in the office and had a system of punishments for latecomers. He ruled the office with an iron rod. Staff were terrified. And if anyone dared to offer a contrary viewpoint in meetings, they were given the notorious stare. Not the best example in the world of influencing skill!

We guess there is no shortage of characters like that who would prefer to simply dish out orders. They think that unless they wield the big stick, no one will take any notice.

Things Are Different Now

Times have changed, though. People don't take too kindly to being pushed around. That doesn't mean they disobey edicts from on high, but they probably don't give their best if they are simply bossed around.

That means managers have to think carefully about how to get what they want. Let's face it, all managers need help and support. Some do it pretty well, and they don't need to throw their weight around. You won't hear them saying, "You will do what I say because I am the boss!"

How Do Some Managers Seem to Get Their Way?

The answer to that question is simple. They are accomplished influencers – they have the knack of winning people over. They can influence how others behave. That is exactly what influencing is: getting your way without being bossy.

Why Do Some Not Do So Well?

There are managers between the two extremes who are able to influence people in some situations, but don't do very well in others. That's because they think there are only one or two ways to go about it.

For example, many managers have told us in the past that you will invariably get your way if you give people sound reasons for doing things. That's optimism for you! But don't think because someone says 'yes' he really agrees. Getting someone to nod his head is one thing. Getting commitment is something entirely different.

Many just go about things in the wrong way. Why? Well, to start off, we are all creatures of habit, but sometimes the way we normally like to do things is not the best way.

Another reason may be that these people don't think before they do. In other words, they put action before thought. A recipe for disaster if there ever was one!

Using Muscle As a Last Resort

We were talking to a group of department heads about getting their staff to do things, and they came up with all the right suggestions about being polite and making them feel good about their work. As soon as we asked them what they do if someone refuses a request, even though it may be perfectly reasonable, the answer was invariably, "Order them to do it".

If you don't promote me, I'll tell my mum!

It is true that, if the worst comes to the worst, managers can resort to using their muscle, but even that doesn't always work. It would be asking for big trouble in some settings.

And managers certainly can't throw their weight around with their peers or those upstairs. Imagine shouting at the boss because he won't let you have your way. You may end up studying the classified pages of the local rag with anxious interest!

How Can You Have Your Way But Still Maintain Relationships?

What we are asking is how you can have it both ways. How do you get what you want and stay the best of friends with people at the same time? There is no simple answer. A lot depends on the situation, whether the other person outranks you or not, and the way you normally like to influence others.

One thing needs to be made clear. We can't be good at everything. Some of us are good at using some influencing strategies, and some at others. So when you look at the seven strategies below, don't think you have to be brilliant at them all. Just think about the ones that describe you.

Friendliness

If you use this strategy, you like to be seen as the 'nice guy'. You try to be friendly and smile a lot. If you sense the other person is not in a good mood, you hold off until the right time.

You are aware of people's moods and feelings, and you try to make them feel important. "I know everyone wants you to do things, but if you could do this for me, I'd be really grateful."

> A door-to-door salesman, an able exponent of this strategy, was asked why he was so successful. "Easy," he replied. "Every time a middle aged lady answers the door, I say: 'Excuse me, is your mother in?' "

Don't you get the impression, however, that some people are just too good to be true? This strategy can work well, but be careful not to overuse it. People will become suspicious of your motives.

If used to extremes, it becomes 'crawling'. And we can tell you that 'crawlers' are not the most universally admired people. The lesson is: if you are going to 'butter people up', don't be too obvious about it.

Exchange

This is a strategy children seem to be better at than adults. They swap things with their friends, and they bargain their way with parents for later bedtimes.

You too can strike deals, bargains and compromises, using things like time, money, responsibilities and other benefits. "If you could come in to help out on Saturday, I could let you take Monday off."

Of course, you must have something to bargain with. The story is told about a gunfight in a saloon bar with bullets ricocheting off walls, floor and ceiling. A diminutive man with spectacles walked in, crossed the floor and ordered a drink at the bar. The bartender asked him how he could be so brave. "Oh, they won't shoot me," he replied. "I owe money to the lot of them." He certainly had bargaining power!

You have to be careful, however. If you use the strategy too much, people will expect something every time. Also, bear in mind that some people can get pretty greedy, and that can lead to a lot of ill feeling.

Reasoning

If you use this strategy, you are one of life's thinkers and planners. You work things out in your mind before opening your mouth. You also like to get your facts straight. If you are really clever, you think what the other person's responses are likely to be.

Doing your homework is important. If you don't prepare, it doesn't work. Also, you have to make sure your request is not unreasonable.

Some managers like to use this strategy all the time. But don't overlook the fact that not every situation is governed by reason. We could give some compelling reasons why we should be given an immediate 50 per cent pay rise, for example, but we probably stand more chance of selling ice cubes to Eskimos.

Assertiveness

Assertiveness has been associated unfortunately with being 'pushy' and this can mean people being seen as awkward to deal with. One of our colleagues was actually told not to teach young managers assertiveness, as their bosses were complaining that they were using the word 'no' too often!

Assertiveness can mean getting to the point and being firm, but in this context, it covers a multitude of sins and skills. The sins might include shouting and getting angry. The more positive behaviours are getting straight to the point, being firm, and occasionally 'nagging' so that work gets done well and on time.

Be careful though. You can get up people's noses by being too direct or reminding them about something just once too often. It can be useful, but it can also cause a bit of unpleasantness.

Upward referral

This is not the best strategy in the world, since it may mean going over your boss's head, and he may take none too kindly to that. You may also be seen as a weakling if you go running to your boss whenever your staff won't do what you want. It does no one's self-esteem any good to be seen as a 'cry baby'.

Coalition

Some are good at forming alliances with others and some are hopeless at it. We remember one junior manager, hell-bent on promotion, spending a lot of time getting friendly with the boss. But the latter was given the push, and that effectively put paid to his ambitions.

You have to choose the right people to join forces with if you are going to make this strategy work. You have to know who is worth making friends with and who isn't.

Also, don't assume that the people high up the organisation are always the most powerful. There may be others who have a fair bit of clout. Some of our most humble colleagues are able to mould opinions and decisions.

You need to be fairly careful that you are not seen as a conspirator or that you and your associates are not seen as ganging up on the boss. This could damage relationships irreparably.

Coalition is a political strategy that requires time, skill and effort. It also needs to be used with great discretion. Used properly though, it can be pretty powerful and help you out of some sticky situations.

Sanctions

Remember the boss we told you about earlier – the one who didn't like people breathing at work? He would probably have been fairly handy with this strategy, with his taste for banning this and punishing that.

It is true you may get your way by treating people like naughty schoolchildren, perhaps by withdrawing privileges or giving them the worst work. You may even be a little more subtle and ignore them during meetings or put their desks in the draughtiest spots.

You would, of course, be seen as a nasty piece of work! And you also have to ask yourself whether you really want the unpleasantness that all this causes. Is it really worth it?

Getting It Right

> Chris approached the invariably offhand secretary. "I need this conference paper typed urgently. I'll give you fifty dollars if you can get it done for me."

You could argue he was successful because his work was completed on time. But first of all, he did not have to engage in bribery (*exchange* strategy) since it was part of her job anyway, and secondly, the next time he took some work in, she asked, "What do I get for this?"

This illustrates the need to consider carefully the right strategy for the right situation. Relying too much on a single influencing method may be risky. If you want to be successful, you have to be flexible and able to select the best method for the circumstances.

Even if you are the big boss, you can still learn to use different strategies. It will do you far more good than relying on your grand position power.

There are some pretty useful strategies that work well for

managers at all levels. For example, *reasoning, friendliness, exchange* and *assertiveness* are all good, but you have to choose the right situation to employ them. You can't simply use your favourite one all the time. The art of influencing is too complex for that.

Have You Chosen the Right Strategy?

How do you know if you have chosen the right strategy and used it well? If you can answer 'yes' to the following three questions, you have probably acted wisely:

1. Was the person willing to comply?
2. Was there a genuine commitment from that person?
3. Was a good relationship maintained between the other person and myself?

Relationships are unlikely to be maintained if you frighten, push or punish people. So the third question is very important. You may win a battle, but you are unlikely to win the war. Remember, you have to go on working with these people.

How Do You Become a Successful Influencer?

Where does all this leave you as an influencer? First, can you influence others, or are you one of those who says things like: "I cannot get anyone to do anything here. They're all unwilling to cooperate", or "The boss doesn't understand. I never get the resources to do the job".

Are you one who feels helpless, forever dissatisfied, and incapable of influencing a dog to bark? If you think like this, you'll never get what you want.

You have to be positive and believe that you can make things happen. And you can do that by choosing the right influencing strategies.

Think about the following questions:

1. Do you use whatever strategy you feel like at the time?
2. Do you use just one or two for all situations?
3. Do you avoid using any strategy in some situations for fear of failure?

If you answered 'yes' to any question you may need to think about how you influence people. Don't work on instinct – it can let you down. *Think* about the best strategy. Then plan how to use it.

If you use only one or two strategies, think about using a few more. If you are one of life's bargainers, start using *friendliness* or *assertiveness* a bit more. Then you may not have to give things away every time you want something.

Don't be afraid of failing. We all get it wrong. We ask for help and we don't get it. We ask people to do things and they refuse. When that happens, see it as an opportunity to consider whether you really did use the best strategy, and plan how you can try again using a different approach.

Better Still, How Do You Become an 'Expert' Influencer?

To improve your skills you must learn to be:

♦ flexible, so that you can use different strategies;
♦ skilful at choosing the right one for the situation;
♦ strong on reasoning things out.

The expert influencer is not just a friendly person, or an assertive one, or a brilliant swapper. He has more than one trick up his sleeve. More than that, he knows when to use them. How? He thinks about past experiences, about why he is trying to influence, and about the other person. Some people respond well to the friendly approach. Others think of it as manipulative. So know your people.

The expert influencer is pretty good at quite a few strategies, but he is particularly strong at reasoning things out. He assembles strong arguments and very cleverly works out the benefits to the person he is going to influence.

Finally . . .

Think about the sort of influencer you are. Are you seen as 'bossy boots' and do you simply dish out commands to be obeyed? Are you flexible or are you only able to use one or two strategies, whatever the occasion? Do you ever think before you try to influence someone and consider how you might best get your way, whilst keeping good relationships? And finally, while you may be a warm person and smooth talker, or good at using other strategies, how skilful are you at thinking your arguments through in a persuasive and well-reasoned way?

Those who become skilful influencers are successful in getting what they want, but they still ensure the workplace is a happy and productive place for people to enjoy their working lives.

Improving Your Influencing Skill

♦ Develop skill in at least three or four strategies.
♦ *Think* first and then use the one you think is most likely to work.
♦ If you get commitment from the other person and you still have a good relationship, you have done well.
♦ Become good at reasoning things out, but ensure you do your homework properly.

CHAPTER 15

Getting Ready for the Weekly Pow-wow

Ask people what they dread most about their working lives and we can guarantee that meetings will figure prominently. That's no surprise. Many meetings demanding our presence have been nothing short of torture. Apart from the discomfort, most meetings fail to achieve very much. See if your experience is anything like the following accounts of the meeting malady.

Poor Meetings

Why are we here?

Have you ever been to a meeting where there is nothing important to discuss but the meeting takes place anyway, often because: "We always have a meeting on Wednesday afternoon"? You may even be the person who organises these events.

Meetings are often held because, through some warped reasoning, managers think people enjoy them or are used to having them. Such forums too easily become avenues for escaping real work. If you insist on holding a meeting simply for maintaining espirit de corps, you are probably better off organising a knees-up at the pub.

What do you mean?

Poor meetings tend to complicate even the simplest affairs. Meetings were never designed to deal with the trivial things that could be handled easily by one person. So when you put several people together to discuss whether the cleaner should be given a red or a blue brush, do not be surprised when someone talks for fifteen minutes about the cost savings of buying yellow plastic-coated ones.

Wake me up when it's over!

Have you ever been to a meeting that finished early? If you have, you are one of the lucky ones. They're not that easy to remember. Meetings that run over time are not easy to recall either, since most people use them to catch up on lost sleep. They do it with their eyes open!

Here he goes again!

The particularly annoying character is the one who loves the sound of his own voice: "Oh no, here he goes again." The chairperson has probably made the mistake of asking whether anyone has an opinion. This is often the cue for the professional opinion-giver to air his views, usually with the expenditure of large volumes of breath. He leaves the meeting feeling satisfied that he has exercised his larynx, the chairperson thinks there has been commendable involvement, and the remainder of the group have completed enough crosswords or doodles to fill a book.

At least they always leave the weekly meeting refreshed.

Let's decide later

Another common fault in meetings is to put decisions off. If the meeting is designed to arrive at a decision, then this is what should happen before it ends. Decisions tend to be avoided because the issues become complicated. The chairperson has failed to keep control of discussions and draw contributions together so that the issue remains clear in everybody's mind. One wonders how much productivity is sacrificed because decisions have been passed from meeting to meeting without action.

How often have you left a meeting and the only thing which has been decided is when the next meeting will be held? Good meetings produce decisions and actions. Members should leave with something to do. There should be plans for action.

Most poor meetings, like those above, are the result of poor planning. A bit of thought can have a remarkable effect on the success of a meeting. Let's now look at how to prepare for meetings. First, however, we'll introduce you to Joan, an up-and-coming human resource manager from a medium sized telecommunications company.

Meeting Joan

When Joan holds a dinner party, our guess is that she waits for her guests to arrive, then starts thinking about what she should put on the menu, and then frantically calls the caterer to bring it over. Ridiculous? To be honest, we don't know what she does at home, but if she organises things the same way she manages her department, we are probably not far off the mark.

For example, she was the last to arrive for the weekly meeting. She claimed it was because of a traffic hold-up on the ring road. But everyone knew she had probably been in her office puzzling over what she should put on the agenda. It was the same every week. She would rush in late, mumble an apology and start talking about anything which came to mind at the time. Of course, they had important things to discuss, but since they usually spent most of the time dealing with relatively trivial matters, they seldom got round to these. What had they discussed over the previous few weeks?

1. Which hotel visiting consultants should use.
2. Who would be able to have time off at New Year.
3. Who was going to do the sales reps' typing.
4. What the shortest route to the plant in Woodlands was.
5. What needed to be done at the next meeting.

Not the most productive example of company meetings! The pity was that Joan was generally a very capable manager, bright, keen and dedicated. She was just hopeless when it came to preparing for meetings – they were more like social gatherings than business forums.

Joan is not alone. As we know all too well, many managers seem to have difficulty in preparing adequately for meetings. Poorly planned, they are a waste of time; time needed to thrash out the things that count. Fortunately, there are a number of fairly simple steps that can be taken to overcome the problem.

Be Prepared

What's it all about?

The first step is to decide the purpose of the meeting. It amazes us how many people call a meeting without really thinking about why. Imagine organising your holiday by getting in the car and seeing where you end up. Not a bad idea if you like surprises in life, but the surprise may be an unpleasant one if you end up in the wrong place. With a bit of forethought, you could arrive at a location you enjoy.

Similarly, with meetings, you need to prepare by asking yourself a number of questions about the necessity and purpose of the meeting.

- What do I want the meeting to achieve?
- Is it to share information, make a placement decision or discuss future direction?
- Can the purpose be achieved in another way (by memo or telephone)?
- Do I need to be involved at the meeting?
- Will the meeting be worth the time invested?

As we mentioned above, it is certainly not unusual for meetings to be held every Tuesday morning just because they have always been held then. If this is the only reason for having the meeting, it is probably as useful as a sandpit to a Bedouin.

Suppose you have decided that the meeting will be useful and necessary, you then need to turn your attention to who should attend.

Who should come?

The old maxim 'time is money' is true, and you may be throwing plenty of it away if you have people at the meeting who don't need to be there. Remember, a meeting is not a cocktail party where people gather just 'to be seen' or to engage in the latest gossip.

A general rule of thumb is 'the fewer, the merrier'. The larger the gathering, the more unwieldy it is. These are the key questions when you are deciding who should be there:

♦ Do they have control of relevant resources?
♦ Are they knowledgeable about the issue?
♦ Do they have special skills that can be used?
♦ Is a certain person's status important to what can be achieved?
♦ What can they contribute to the expected outcomes of the meeting?

Ideally, each person who attends the meeting should have something to offer. If they just come along for their weekly snooze, do them and yourself a favour – let them slumber at their own desks.

What to expect

You have to let people know in advance what the idea of the meeting is. Write to them stating in one sentence what the meeting hopes to achieve. Then you can elaborate a little. Let them know what you expect of them: for example, you may require them to read relevant documents, gather views from employees, be prepared to discuss issues, and be ready to make a decision.

Ensure everybody is prepared for the meeting. There is no point in people voicing their opinions if they have not done their homework.

Write it down

Prepare an agenda and consider thoughtfully the order of items and time available for each. There will always be some items that should be discussed before others, so place them high on the agenda. Ensure you allow time to discuss the really important issues and give little time to the less critical items. It is sometimes useful to put trivial items at the top of the agenda, but restrict the time you spend on them. Actually write the starting and finishing time for each item and try to stick to it.

The one-liners you usually see are not really agendas but crib sheets so the chairman can remember what comes next. A real agenda has a short explanation of each item and indicates what the outcome might be. Take care when compiling an agenda. Deal with only a limited number of issues.

Not too long, please!

"What's your job?"
"I'm secretary of the chess club," the man replied.
"What do you have to do?"
"I read the hours of the last meeting."

How many of the meetings we are involved in are like that, measured in hours rather than minutes? They can be made shorter in the first place by limiting the number of agenda items. A forty-two item agenda may indeed represent a participative style of management. It may also reveal a complete lack of understanding of what meetings are really for. One manager actually did this. His staff could have sat through three General Election campaigns in the time it must have taken to deal with the items even superficially. If your agenda looks more like a telephone directory, a bit of surgery is called for!

Preparation does not finish when you enter the meeting arena. It is important to use the first few minutes to reinforce the purpose.

Make it clear

At the beginning of the meeting, go through the purpose, the agenda and the allocated time for each item. Everyone will then understand your priorities. Restate the purpose of the meeting and what you expect to have achieved by the time it is finished – these become your guides for action. When you are sure everybody understands, you can press on.

Under control

One final point on preparation. As chairperson, you are responsible for controlling the meeting. Your planning should attempt to predict and deal with disruptive influences. Earlier, for example, we mentioned the 'I love my own voice' individual who can wipe out the usefulness of a meeting with his ill-timed soliloquy. Sure, such people often have something useful to contribute. But the Chair's job is to get them to say it before the sun goes down.

Think of ways of containing displays of enthusiasm and people's tendency to waffle on about anything other than the agenda item. Perhaps give them a set time in which to speak and then move on to the next person. It works wonders.

Finally . . .

If you can follow these simple pointers, you will give yourself at least a sporting chance of running a successful and productive meeting.

Thorough preparation can save a lot of headache during meetings. Of course, you still need a fair bit of skill to keep the meeting running well. For example, you should be able to summarise people's comments, keep the discussion on track, stick to time, and move towards purposeful decisions. But if you haven't prepared properly, these will be of little use to you anyway.

So, don't be like Joan. Do your homework. Think about it carefully, and you'll be amazed at the difference in terms of efficiency, productivity and morale. Make your meetings worth the organisational time they consume. That should make everyone a lot happier.

How to Improve Your Meeting Preparation Skills

♦ Think carefully about *why* you need a meeting.
♦ Only have people there who can contribute to achieving the purpose.
♦ Write to people in advance explaining the purpose of the meeting.
♦ Insist on people doing their homework before the meeting.
♦ Distribute an agenda a day or two in advance – only a few items, with each one explained.
♦ Allocate plenty of time to the important items.
♦ At the beginning of the meeting, clarify the purpose and state time limits for the items and the meeting's finishing time.
♦ Try to anticipate any disruptive influences and plan how to deal with them.

CHAPTER 16

Getting to Grips With Conflict

When most people think of conflict, it conjures up negative images of bitter fights, prolonged arguments and unpleasant exchanges. The general opinion is that any type of conflict should be avoided like the plague. True, some of the acrimonious exchanges we witness between individuals can be nasty, but there again, people are not all sweetness and light, as the sergeant below well knew:

> Life had been quiet for the past few days at the police station, so the officers put their feet up and enjoyed a few games of cards. "This is boring," said one. "No violence, no robberies, no murders, no nothin'."
> "Don't worry," said the sergeant. "Things will come alive soon. Just have faith in human nature."

How Fights Start

Conflicts and even verbal fights can start in any number of ways. We are not much different from children in this respect. It's just that, as we get older, we learn to control ourselves a bit better. Let's look briefly at some of the common ways that conflicts begin.

What do you mean?

> "The regulation does not mean we have to be here until 4.30 pm. It's only a guide. After all, we are supposed to be professionals."
> "If it says 4.30, it means 4.30. If the paper says the news is on at 6.30, I suppose you think you can switch on at 9 pm?"

Many conflicts arise from misunderstandings or different interpretations. These are usually the result of poor communication. Such initially harmless conflicts can turn nasty if one or both parties start to use the 'wrong' words or phrases when voicing their opinions. A friend of ours calls them 'hot button' words: use them at the wrong time and watch the flames rise!

I don't like you

Jose: I can't agree with Leo on that one. I think we would be better . . .

Leo: Here we go again. Wasn't it enough that you humiliated me and my staff over the Belgrave account? I'm getting sick and tired of your pumped-up sense of importance and the way . . .

Jose: Now wait just a minute my friend. I was trying to have a perfectly reasonable discussion and . . .

Leo: Rubbish, you're always trying to . . .

It doesn't always need an event or issue to provoke a conflict. Emotional conflict, for example, can be caused by people's deep-seated personal feelings about one another. Emotions tend to last longer than any particular conflict-initiating event.

Can't agree

Conflicts also arise, of course, from people having different viewpoints. Such conflicts are often about goals. For example, one employee may believe that stock levels should be kept high in order to service customers rapidly, whereas another may see that as a waste of resources and wish to keep costs down by maintaining stock levels to a minimum.

What's important?

Jean: In my opinion, it is our obligation to promote more women into management positions. It's about time we kept up with the rest of the world and did away with this old boys' network. You must all acknowledge that women do a better, more caring job than men.

Roland: I've got nothing against women managers, but I am against any suggestion that we should promote people on the basis of gender. We should do it on merit and nothing else.

Tough one! People's values are reflections of their personality and what they believe, and as such, they are difficult, if not impossible in some cases, to change. At times, values are really the root cause of conflict situations which may, on the surface, appear to have other causes. Differences in values and beliefs can cause much suspicion, misunderstanding, and hostility.

Positive or Negative Conflict

Conflict is a dirty word in many organisations. They go so far as telling you it doesn't exist. However, we haven't found a set-up yet where there is no conflict, and that includes business organisations, public sector operations and even churches.

As the police sergeant rightly observed, there is no doubt that human nature, being what it is, will ensure that conflict arises. But it doesn't always have to be destructive. In fact, correctly guided conflict can be a valuable source of creativity, so it is best not to waste time trying to eliminate it. On the contrary, it is more productive to promote the right type of conflict and harness the outcomes for the organisation's benefit.

You may ask how conflict can ever be productive. Imagine you are in a meeting called to discuss the future direction of your unit. The unit head has thrown a few ideas together of how she sees the future and presents them to the group. Everyone just sits and mumbles, "Looks fine to me"; "I agree"; "Whatever you say". No disagreement, no dissent, no conflict – what sort of future plan do you think the group will end up with?

Think about how much more productive such a get-together would be if the staff openly challenged the boss's and one another's ideas: "But that would mean...."; "I disagree, could we try...."; or "There must be a better way to do it". There can be little doubt that richer, more productive ideas would flow, provided disagreement did not get out of hand.

The trick for managers is to encourage productive conflict and reduce destructive conflict, to foster the positive outcomes of disagreement and minimise the more unwelcome effects.

Now let's look at some of the ways managers typically deal with conflict.

Turn the Other Way

How do people typically cope or deal with conflict? Some simply avoid it, look the other way, and hope that when they turn round it has disappeared. Although this can work sometimes, you run the risk of being seen as fairly gutless. It is unlikely to do much good when there are damaging interpersonal conflicts around.

The boss likes to tell people he has never seen anyone fall out in this office.

Turning your back on conflict can be done in a number of ways. One well-known strategy is to put it off: "How about we decide who should get the car tomorrow, if I have time?" Another way is to ignore it:

> "Jason just said the work I have been doing for the last six months is worthless. I want this settled."
> "I'm sure it will sort itself out. Now, what did you think of the game last night?"

A further strategy used is to isolate the conflicting parties and hope they get over it. One of the big weaknesses of this strategy is that you can't keep people apart indefinitely, especially if you are trying to increase your use of teams.

Do What You Like

Other managers take the easy way out and give in to any demand in order to avoid conflict. This is OK if you want to lose out and be seen as a pushover. There is also a limit to how many times and to how many people you can give in. Conflicts will only intensify.

Furthermore, demands may change:

"Look, I've been thinking about our disagreement."
"Well?"
"I've decided to go along with your idea after all."
"You have, have you? Well, I've changed my mind."

Stop It!

Another strategy which seems to be used all too often is the 'order them to stop' approach. In short, taking on the role of dictator and 'ordering' your way out of conflict.

Do this all the time, and people will go into their shells and keep their ideas to themselves. That does no one any good. Productivity can suffer and the damage can be difficult to repair.

If you use your authority muscle to squash conflict, you win and the other guy loses. Good for you, maybe, but not the best prescription for gaining commitment.

Meet You Half Way

A widely used strategy is that of compromise: give and take. "Let's look for the easy way out (even if it is a mediocre solution to the problem)." In this approach conflicting parties are asked to make certain sacrifices in exchange for some concessions from the other – for the good of the company. Each party wins some and loses some.

This is a fairly common strategy and one that has considerable merit, but it is not risk-free. If used too frequently, for example, the leader may be seen as someone who is more interested in simply keeping everyone happy than in solving problems. Compromise for the sake of compromise should not be the aim.

Let's Work Together

Perhaps the best way of all of arriving at a good solution is to promote a collaborative problem-solving culture within the organisation: to get people working together on problems rather than against one another in constant competition. Approaching conflict collaboratively aims for *win–win* rather than *win–lose* situations.

It means focusing on problems rather than personalities. It also means confronting the problem and not sweeping it under the carpet. Furthermore, it means working together and nudging the old brain for a bit of creativity. Without doubt, this is the most powerful strategy for turning destructive conflicts into constructive outcomes.

How do you promote this sort of approach? First, you have to make communication open and constructive. None of those sneaky remarks behind people's backs. And you have to get people talking to one another, tackling problems head-on. This way, they can understand one another's point of view better. They don't have to agree, of course. But there's no need for them to fall out either.

That's it in general terms, but how do you create such a collaborative culture? There are several strategies that can help:

Admit and welcome

Welcome and even encourage disagreement in the organisation. View problems as challenges and conflict as an integral part of tackling them. You've got to take risks and be able to accept criticism of the way you do things and also of your ideas. If you show you can't take it, don't expect people to be open with you.

You have to be willing to admit that a problem exists and to bring it into the open. This is a bit different to pretending it doesn't exist and keeping your mouth shut in order to avoid unpleasant scenes. If you don't open things up, they stew in people's minds and then get blown up out of all proportion. The conflict doesn't get solved and the situation gets worse.

Clarify and confront

Make sure you understand the nature of the conflict. Don't underestimate people's feelings. Even if a conflict situation seems petty or meaningless to you, it is very real to those involved. Trivialising people's emotions can produce even more intense, destructive feelings. Just think how it would feel if you were to open up to a friend about a relationship difficulty, and he told you to "grow up, and don't be such a baby"?

The process involves a fair bit of chinwagging. You have to ~uss and explore things, and also look at the strength of people's ~s. Even more important, the process involves listening – plenty

n't forget, you should be discussing the problem, not ~e problem is about things that are being done. Person- ~he people who are doing them. There's a big ~say, "I don't like the way you are approaching ~finitely out of order to say: "You are the sort ~ things up".

137

Get all this right, and the outcome is a better understanding of others' point of view. It's the only way of moving towards a lasting and worthwhile solution.

Establish

Set up collaborative mechanisms for dealing with conflict. Develop firm procedures and 'ground rules' for employees to follow, and separate ideas from individuals. Ensure that everyone involved is treated equitably.

There is obviously little point in simply 'saying' you will deal with any disagreements in a collaborative fashion and then not provide the means for people to do so. That would be like telling your kids they are free to play in the backyard and then locking them in the bedroom. You have to arrange communication channels that can be made effective use of.

Not every time

Collaboration is a powerful way of dealing with conflict, but it doesn't always work. For example, if a conflict is based on a serious clash in values, trying to push collaboration can actually polarise differences and is highly unlikely to alter basic beliefs. This, of course, can lead to even more intense disagreement.

Nevertheless, strategies where people work together to tackle conflicting views, opinions and difficulties probably offer the most promise for transforming destructive conflicts into constructive, creative outcomes.

Finally . . .

You can never eliminate conflict, but you can reduce its negative effects and work to achieve potentially constructive outcomes. These will help keep your organisation vibrant and responsive, and prevent both the staleness that comes from the extremes of concord and the destructiveness from freewheeling, distasteful conflict.

How to Deal Properly With Conflict

♦ Try to use collaboration as a way of resolving most conflicts.
♦ Welcome conflicts as challenges and opportunities rather than headaches.
♦ Try to understand the other person's position.
♦ Don't trivialise people's feelings.

- Be prepared to do a lot of listening.
- Stick to issues, not personalities.
- Set up collaborative mechanisms for dealing with conflict.
- Build open communication channels into your structure for people to access if conflicts arise.

Manager

CHAPTER 17

Attacks By Time Thieves
How to Defend Yourself

One manager was so obsessive about conserving resources he stopped his watch to save time!

A study conducted in the United States showed that the average person spends five years of his or her life waiting in lines, three years sitting in meetings, four years shifting priorities and one year searching through clutter. After reading that, there didn't seem to be much point in forking out a fortune on a country club membership – there wouldn't be time to make use of it!

Well, country club memberships have increased in value, but time, for most people, seems to go the other way. They have less and less of it. Of course, most want to indulge in leisure and spend some time with their families, but it seems to be in increasingly short supply. Why?

When you look carefully at how managers in particular spend their time, there is one thing that comes to the fore frequently. It never ceases to amaze us how the little, seemingly insignificant things literally steal the time from right under our noses. Time that we can never get back.

In this chapter, we shall look at what are best called *time thieves* and suggest some ways in which you can arrest them. Think about your own life. You can probably recognise these kleptomaniacs and how you yourself have been frequently robbed by them.

Outside and Inside Thieves

There are two basic types of thieves. One type can be labelled outside thieves, those that appear in the guise of long and unwanted telepho

Don't bother me with the strategic marketing plan now.
Can't you see I'm tied up?

calls and visitors, unstructured meetings, interpersonal conflicts among staff, and idle talk.

The other type, *inside thieves*, come from inside and may include an inability to say 'no', indecision, putting things off till tomorrow, guilt, inability to plan and prioritise, and poor delegation skills.

Like most people, you have almost certainly been attacked by both types of thieves. Let's look a little more closely at four of these little `ighters, probably the most common ones we all encounter.

Let's Do It Later

`icularly insidious. He says things like, "Why don't you
`elax, you've got plenty of time". Strangely enough,
`de with tasks that are particularly important or
`ajor decision needs to be made. He rarely
`rity, easy or pleasant tasks are around.

He also encourages you to have plenty of social chats when the work is piling up, to go through your mail yet again, and to tidy your already meticulously neat desk.

How many times have you said to yourself: "I'll start that task tomorrow; I don't have time now"? John F. Kennedy once stated, "We must use time as a tool, not as a couch." If you put off the important, your work won't have much impact.

Break it up, take it up, and do it now

In fairness, we are all a bit weak-kneed when it comes to doing the difficult things. What can you do about it? If you are faced with a daunting task, and you are not too keen on starting it, break it up into small pieces and tackle one at a time. Set yourself a target of spending five minutes on it *today*.

Starting is always the difficult part. Once you are underway, it gets easier. Like a sculptor gets to work on a big piece of rock with his hammer and chisel, you can chip away at that formidable task. It's surprising how quickly it will start to take shape.

And one further thing – very important – reward yourself when you have completed one part. That tends to work for most of us.

Of course, most of us would rather sort the paper clips in the right coloured piles than start a tricky project. So discipline yourself. Set a start time for that important task, and stick to it. You'll feel better about yourself.

Do it *now*. As the famous playwright Arthur Miller wrote: "The word 'now' is like a bomb through the window, and it ticks." Don't wait till it explodes. Try to replace the 'let's do it later' thoughts with a 'do it now' attitude.

And as a final word on procrastination, heed this warning: never finish anything you haven't started!

That's Not Good Enough

Joe Dove, Unit Head at Tri-Vial Ltd, took great pride in the reports that went out of his department. He considered himself an expert on detecting even the most minor mistakes in any piece of writing: small grammatical and typographical errors, even the quality of the print. It was nothing for him to spend the entire morning putting someone's work under the microscope. He never made any comment on the content of the reports but he was like a bull terrier if a comma was in the wrong place. There were rumours that he even corrected the graffiti in the bathrooms! He encouraged his staff to spend as much time necessary on reports to get them perfect before he took to them with poison red pen.

Let's not knock Joe for expecting a good job, but maybe he needed to ask himself if the time he committed to relatively trivial matters was what a manager should be doing. His all-consuming addiction to the perfect report was really a waste of valuable time.

If you are like Joe, you may either end up doing everything yourself, because you believe you are the only person capable of such perfection, or you may alienate and frustrate employees and colleagues alike, because what they do will never be good enough.

Joe had the perfectionism bug. His obsessive attention to detail stopped him from going further up the ladder. He avoided delegating, rarely asked for assistance (because he knew he'd have to do it again himself), and was constantly asking his boss to extend deadlines "just to get it absolutely right". If you spend all your time on the finer points of detail, you may have little time left for the things that really matter.

Broaden the view

Overcoming excessive perfectionism requires keeping an eye on the 'big picture': What you are there for. Sure, it's permissible to concentrate on some details, but not when they prevent you from doing what you are paid to do.

To avoid getting bogged down in trivia, you have to prioritise your work. Don't spend time trying to perfect low priority tasks. Ask yourself one simple question: Does the time commitment justify the quality and quantity of the output?

To be effective, speed is sometimes as vital as accuracy. Prioritise your actions, trust others to complete tasks, and concentrate on what is really important.

You Never Told Me

Another thief who will do all he can to steal your time is the 'you never told me' or 'how was I meant to know?' character. He thrives in offices or organisations that are not communication-conscious.

Zac was extremely pleased with himself. He had got rid of Pauline and managed to track down a top-class replacement from a rival company. it would cost a bomb, but he knew this person would fit the bill. uldn't believe his boss's reaction when he proudly announced d done. Zac said, "But you sent me the memo. Look, it says, ting waves. Better get someone new – and quick.' "

explained that he meant to get someone new for the Pauline with the Howard and Cosgrove account. hes: he couldn't afford the new guy and Pauline ck up a legal fuss.

If your employees don't know what is expected, they will either be continually harassing you to find out what they should be doing or, as in Zac's case, doing the wrong thing.

Too often, the wrong medium of communication is used. Writing memos to someone in the next office is silly, especially if the matter is complex. In other situations, putting things in writing may be the right thing to do.

Poor communication wastes a lot of time. Why tell your staff individually the same thing seventeen times over? Why not get them together for a few minutes or put a notice on the board? Get your communication right, and you can save yourself a lot of time.

Know what I mean?

Think about what you have to communicate and decide which medium is most suitable: meeting, telephone, bulletin board, face-to-face conversation, memo and so on. Match the level of communication to those involved and the complexity of the task.

Take care, however, not to over-communicate. Clarity, not volume is the key word. If you are asking someone to carry out a specific task, provide only the information he needs.

You should also be able to feed information into the system quickly and simply, and know it will reach its destination in understandable form. Use simple language. If you have to meet, then fine, but don't waste people's time without good reason. Group meetings are sometimes necessary in order to brief people and then to make sure they understand.

Interrupt Me, Please

> "Just thought I'd drop in to say hello. Can't seem to work today. Could I trouble you for a coffee?"

It happens all the time, but usually when you are knee-deep in work. In the same way people leave windows open and doors unlocked, it is our own fault when this thief takes advantage of our generosity.

Many managers extend an open invitation to the thief by having an 'open-door' policy. "My door is always open. Feel free to come and see me whenever you like." That is a way of telling everyone that your time and job are unimportant. Is that what you are really trying to say?

Even without the dreaded open door, the thief will attack by arranging for a constant stream of unplanned visitors and interruptions. The thief is not stupid. He goes for those who don't have any plans for dealing with disturbances. He also sends the most talkative visitors to managers who find it impossible to terminate a conversation.

Restrict, screen and control

The first step in controlling interruptions is to start sending an entirely different message to your colleagues. Think about instituting a limited open-door policy, perhaps encouraging colleagues to come and see you on Tuesday afternoons between 2 pm and 4 pm. But let them know they are welcome only if there is something to discuss. The weather and the state of the economy in Afghanistan do not count.

Of course there are exceptions. You have to be flexible. If someone has a personal problem, he shouldn't have to wait until Tuesday afternoon. But using something like this as a general guide helps.

If you have a secretary, you can set up a screening process so that you are not interrupted by the casual visitor. If you don't, insist on appointments.

Despite all this, you are still bound to get the unwanted visitor from time to time. You can't spare the time, but you don't want to sour relationships by turfing them out. "Get lost, Mike. I haven't got time to waste on you!" may not be the best way of retaining a healthy relationship. However, there's nothing to stop you saying, "I'm tied up now, Mike. Let's fix a time when we can talk".

If you have a choice, meet in someone else's office – it's easier to leave. If people do penetrate the inner sanctuary, stand up when they come in. That way, they won't become too comfortable. Those are useful tricks, and they work!

As a general principle, be ruthless with your time, but gracious with people. After all, you still have to work with them, and any animosity created could lead to wasting even more time. Be polite, get them to the point quickly, and say 'No' if that is what you mean. Then get back to what you are supposed to be doing.

Lock Them Up

Of course, there are many other time thieves. Each of us is more vulnerable to some than others. For example, some of us are suckers when it comes to putting things off until tomorrow. Others are incessantly tempted by the social life. What is important is that we are aware of where our weaknesses lie.

Unfortunately, many don't even realise when the thieves are doing their work. As long as we feel busy during the day and exhausted when we get home, we think we've had a productive day.

So, before you start thinking about how you can devote more of your precious time to the really important aspects of your job, find out how you currently spend your time. You can't lock up the thieves until you know who they are.

One way of finding out is to keep a diary of everything that happens for a whole day – and we mean everything. Write down the time against each event. That way, you should spot where things might be going astray. Another way is to get someone to shadow you and keep a log.

Tracking your time can create a few surprises. One manager discovered he spent nearly three hours a day talking to individuals about all sorts of things, many of them unrelated to work. He had to do some serious thinking about regaining control.

Finally . . .

To lock up those time thieves, find out how and to what extent they are affecting your job. Work out ways of controlling them, actually do it, and then keep an eye on them in case they try to return.

We said earlier one of key lessons in managing your time is to 'do it now'. It's pretty good advice, but it sometimes backfires:

> The managing director was a stickler for getting on with things. He decided one day to hang signs all over the building saying *Do It Now*. By the end of the afternoon, his deputy quit, his secretary ran off with the sales manager, and the security guard stole the company van!

How to Get the Better of Time Thieves

♦ Don't put off important tasks. Try to develop a *do it now* mentality and do important tasks first.

♦ When faced with a daunting task, break it up into smaller, more manageable pieces, and then get stuck into one of them.

♦ Get your priorities right. Don't waste time on trivial things.

♦ Keep your eye on the big picture, and don't get distracted by excessive detail.

♦ Trust others to do the job.

♦ Make your communication simple and appropriate.

♦ Don't make the mistake of over-communicating.

♦ Control the time when people can interrupt you by setting aside specific times and having a screening process.

♦ Be polite but firm with unwanted visitors.

♦ Identify the time thieves you are most vulnerable to and plan ways of beating them.

CHAPTER 18

Writing Management Reports

As Gallagher, in his book *Report Writing for Management* written a quarter of a century ago, aptly put it: "To anyone who has had to prepare a report, it should come as no surprise that many people look forward to writing reports with all the enthusiasm they reserve for an attack of appendicitis. Because writing is painful, they try to avoid it. When they can't avoid it, they postpone it, evidently hoping that if they ignore the task long enough it will go away like a psychosomatic pain."

How seriously do you treat the writing of a management report? We knew from past experience when we wrote this chapter that many managers would be interested in things like leadership and participatory decision making, but when it comes to report writing, their attitude is, "Anything will do – it's only a trivial concern".

We don't think so. The way you write your reports could be a lot more important than you might think. To start off, the quality of the report may be seen as an indication of the quality of the recommendations it makes or the information it provides.

That is important enough in itself, but even more significant is the fact that you, the writer, may be judged on the report. In some cases, promotion may hinge on it.

Whatever type of report you have to write, there are some common principles that can be applied. If you work with these, you can make sure that your works of art get the message across and achieve what they are supposed to achieve.

How to Get Ready to Write the Report

Like many things in management, preparation is the key to effective report writing. Before putting pen to paper, you will (of course) have done your background work, read appropriate documents, assembled information and reached some tentative conclusions about any proposals you might wish to make.

You need to consider several points. First, you have to decide on the purpose. For example, is it to recommend changes, to provide facts, or to record progress? This needs to be clear.

Second, you need to decide what information is required and then obtain it. Acquire only what is relevant. Forget all the other rubbish; it serves merely to confuse matters.

Third, give yourself time to assimilate the information and don't be too hasty in reaching conclusions. It is best not to rush the old grey matter. Things tend to become a bit clearer after a couple of days.

Finally, prepare some arguments and think about conclusions and the recommendations you might make. These are not final, and when you come to put pen to paper, you may well change your mind. Nevertheless, it is a good idea to have some provisional thoughts on outcomes and these will help to focus your report.

Here is my report on the usage of paper clips in the typing pool.

Getting the Message Across

The best advice we can give is to learn to tell a good story! If the report is disjointed with ideas all over the place, it will definitely *not* make compulsive reading. So try to develop a neat storyline.

But it's a special kind of storyline, where you give the reader the ending. That's right. Put the end at the front: 'hit' the reader with the best bits right away. We know it sounds cockeyed, but it works. If your recommendations form the crucial part, then put them at the beginning.

Managers with other things on their minds don't want suspense. Nor do they want detailed logical argument. They want to know the final score. You can't be sure, after all, that the busy reader is going to plough through your *piece de resistance* to the bitter end. So if he reads only one page, make sure it is the right one.

This can be done, of course, in the 'executive summary', which for many managers is the only part of the report to be read! Whether you like it or not, that is reality. You won't find many of the top guys reading every word of your treatise like a Jeffrey Archer novel. So, if you have something to say, say it early.

The exception to this is where you have some bad news. It is probably expedient to build up to your explanation of why the inventory system your boss designed is an unworkable disaster!

What Should the Report Look Like?

If you open one of your own reports, what does it look like? Is it visually boring or attractive? Don't underestimate the impact of your page layout. Many readers are put off by scripts that look like doctoral dissertations.

To make it appealing, you need short paragraphs, good spacing, plenty of sub-headings and lists of ideas where they are appropriate. You don't need to use extra paper. If you write concisely and decide what is important and what isn't, you will actually use less paper, which should incur the profound gratitude of the recipient.

If you work carefully on the visual side, it can do the work for the reader. He doesn't have to think too much about how ideas relate to one another: it is done through the layout. Don't try to use up every square millimetre of the page, since this again is visually off-putting. Leave wide margins so that the reader can make notes.

What Is the Best Style to Use?

We all have different styles of writing. This is a good thing. Some styles are more attractive than others. Whilst we may never achieve the style prowess of our illustrious novelist friends, there are some things we can do.

To begin with, we can do our level best to get the message across clearly. One way is to use short words, short sentences and short paragraphs. You can see how the experts do this by picking up a newspaper. If newspapers were not easy to read, they wouldn't sell. Simple as that.

Perhaps we think we appear clever if we use long words. The principle for management report writing, however, is: don't use long words where short ones will do. In fact, a colleague of ours maintains another expression for 'using short words' is 'growing up'. There is some truth in that.

We have nightmares about some of the academic journals we have to read: some authors probably hold competitions to see who can find the longest and most obscure words, and who can make their writing the most unintelligible.

The same message applies to sentences. The use of short, simple sentences is more effective than elaborate prose. This needs lots of time and practice.

Similarly, paragraphs should be short. Try to put the main idea in the first sentence. This creates the impact for the rest of the paragraph. If you find difficulty in dismantling paragraphs, a quick glance at the newspaper will show how it is done.

How to Make Your Report Clear

A former boss used to say: "Write me a report on your recommendations – on one side of A4 please." That was the limit of his attention span.

Not all reports can be one page long, of course, but it is true that short reports have more impact than weighty volumes. And don't let anyone ever persuade you that quantity equals quality: it doesn't. For our money, it is often the other way round.

> A novice reporter was instructed by his editor to write an important story in 600 words. The novice said, "Impossible. It will take at least double that."
>
> "Remember," said the editor, "the creation was told in 600 words. Try it!"

So, wherever possible, keep your reports short and sweet, by pruning them and leaving only the essential information, concisely written.

It is usually best to avoid using meaningless expressions like 'many' and 'good'. You should also avoid imprecision when the facts are available. For example, in this phrase: 'an enormous drop in revenue', what does 'enormous' mean? It is better to say that 'revenue fell by 20 per cent last year'. Aim, therefore, to answer the questions an informed reader would ask.

It is also best to avoid unnecessary jargon. Some people, however, become tied down by it. As one young man said when he went to the pharmacy:

> "I want some monoaceticacidester of salicyclicacid."
> "You mean aspirin?" asked the pharmacist.
> "That's it! I can never remember the name," replied the young man.

Focus on facts, pure and unadorned. They should be presented simply and clearly. Then you can interpret and colour them with your own views. We think it is good to have a section set aside in management reports for the facts and findings, presented clearly. Any discussion can follow later.

Recommendations in particular should be absolutely clear. They stand little chance of success if they are vague. It is a good idea to type the recommendation statement in bold characters (or underline) and then give a few lines of explanation. But make sure the reader knows precisely what action he should take and when he should take it. Leave him in no doubt.

How to Lay Out Your Report

Now we need to look briefly at the way in which the 'story' unfolds. The report needs a structure. You will find plenty of advice in books about structuring reports, but we prefer not to be too pedantic. As a guide, you must tell your reader:

- what you intended to do originally;
- what you actually did;
- what you found out;
- what you made of your discoveries;
- the conclusions you reached;
- your recommendations.

Even simpler than that, some experts on report writing offer the good advice:

- tell 'em what you are going to tell 'em;
- tell 'em;
- tell 'em what you told 'em.

This is a useful way of thinking about your writing in three phases. Outline what you are going to cover in the report. In other words, provide a summary of the key points. (Don't forget to outline your main recommendations, if you have any.) Then write the report (this will cover the bulk of the document). At the end, go over the main points again. This may sound repetitive and tedious, but it works.

If you follow this format, it will help you in your storytelling. You will explain what the point of the story is and then set the scene. You will go on to outline the problem with some supporting information. Then you will relate what you found when you entered the 'maze' and what you made of it. Finally, you will reach some conclusions, possibly followed by some advice about how to make a better story!

What Is There to Do When It's Finished?

When you have finished writing your report, your job is not over. If you are given an important document to write, it may take up to several days to knock it into shape.

Don't be too hasty. You must show that you are meticulous about accuracy, both of the information and in the presentation. A report which has false data lacks credibility and so does the author! If someone in a meeting shows your facts are wrong, your report will at least lose its impact and may even be discarded.

Presentation is equally important. We learnt this lesson once from a colleague who was giving his opinion on a paper we had prepared for a prestigious journal. With a bold, red pen, he circled all the blemishes as a result of the faulty photocopier. The text was untouched! So take heed. Even the seemingly trivial things can spoil the presentation.

Spelling mistakes and typographical errors may not be quite so serious but they are very distracting for the reader. If you know you have a spelling weakness, get someone else to check the report or do a spell check on the word processor. It is not good enough to blame the secretary's inadequacies for mistakes in an important report. You have to check it out yourself.

How to Sharpen Your Report Even More

This is now the time to cut the 'waffle'! If you have any irrelevant information there, take it out. Ask yourself again: 'What is really important?' You may have to be quite ruthless. It is worth going through this self-torment, however, as it will help to sharpen your report.

Does Your Report Make Sense?

If the report is an important one, you may have to let someone who is not familiar with your work read it, and ask him to mark those parts which are not absolutely clear the first time he reads them. You have to accept you may have to do a bit of rewriting. What is crystal clear to our eminently intelligent eyes may appear somewhat muddy and confused to our intended readership.

Finally . . .

A report tells people a lot about the author. If you want to be seen as scatterbrained, then write off-the-cuff, without any logical sequencing of ideas, and omit odd bits of critical information here and there.

If, on the other hand, you make your reports clear, to the point and comprehensive, you will be seen as someone who can make sense out of confusion, a manager with an ordered mind.

How to Write Reports That Get Read

♦ Decide what the purpose of the report is and gather your information.
♦ Construct a good storyline.
♦ Put a summary that highlights your recommendations at the beginning.
♦ Make it look good: plenty of spacing and subheadings.
♦ Use short words, short sentences and short paragraphs.
♦ Put in only essential information and keep the report short.
♦ Present facts simply and clearly. Then you can discuss them.
♦ Check it for accuracy when it's finished.
♦ Ask someone to read it to ensure it makes sense.

CHAPTER 19

Presenting Your Ideas in Public

"The relationship, which I might tentatively venture to aver has not been without a degree of reciprocal utility and even perhaps occasional gratification, is approaching the point of irreversible bifurcation and, to put it briefly, is in the propinquity of its ultimate regrettable termination."

So said Sir Humphrey Appleby in the TV series 'Yes, Prime Minister'. Sir Humphrey, of course, was purposely trying to pull the wool over the minister's eyes by using the most confusing language he could. But we have all heard people like this who don't have the slightest idea what they are putting their audience through.

How often have you sat listening with embarrassment to someone struggling for words, talking in a monotone, or flapping his arms in the most irritating gestures? Let's face it – it isn't easy speaking in public.

There are probably many occasions when you have to make presentations. Some of them are pretty easy, like informing a few workers about something or updating your colleagues. Other occasions may almost paralyse you with terror.

Think of the first time you had to stand up in front of a large group, all anxiously waiting for you to do or say something stupid (or so you believed). Not easy. That's why some people are permanently lousy at it.

Don't think it saves you just because you have something worthwhile to say. It doesn't. Some of the most stunning ideas get lost because they were presented poorly.

Sorry I'm late gentlemen, I'll start my presentation on time management shortly!

You have to learn presentation skill. You need to learn how to gain attention, how to organise your ideas, how to reinforce information, and how to deliver the presentation. The skill is an important one for all managers.

There are three things we need to look at:

1. Preparation
2. Shape
3. Delivery

Doing Your Homework

If you want to be a skilled presenter, you must do your homework. You must be knowledgeable about the topic. If you get questions, for instance, can you answer them? If you are confident, it shows. You will then find the audience on your side.

In getting ready for your presentation, you need to ask yourself several questions. These are concerned with purpose, content, audience, location, time planning and materials. We shall now look at each of these.

What is the purpose of the presentation?

Why are you making it? It must lead to something. This something is the target. Your target, for example, may be to persuade senior management to buy a new computer system.

Next, you need to set some objectives that will help you reach your target. In this example, the objectives may be:

♦ to let them know why the present computer system is not working well;
♦ to get them to agree that money can be saved by buying a new system;
♦ to obtain a commitment to change.

Right, now you have three objectives. They can form the basis for your presentation. In this case, the presenter would inform senior management about present problems. Then he would persuade them that they could save money (and that can be pretty persuasive!). Finally, he would try and persuade them to say 'yes'. So the structure is there already. He has his presentation mapped out.

What should the presentation include?

The answer to this is easy – as little as possible. What does the audience really need to hear? Only include what is relevant. Cut the other stuff, heartbreaking as it is. What's the point in talking about the economy of Third World countries when you are trying to persuade a group of managers to introduce flexitime? Only put in what is essential. If you finish a few minutes early, great! Everyone will be eternally grateful.

What do you want them to take away? We don't mean pieces of paper and free gifts. We mean, what should they be thinking or planning to do? The answer to that question should determine what you include and what you leave out. Just think about this – your audience will absorb only two or three things at best. What do you want those two or three things to be? It's a good idea to write them down.

Who is going to listen to you?

Think about the audience. Are they the bigwigs? What do they know? Are they likely to be supportive or resistant to your ideas? Put yourself in their place and ask yourself what they want to hear. Doing this can make your message come alive.

Where will the presentation be held?

If you have any say in it, choose a comfortable place where there are few distractions. Make sure that everyone can see and hear you clearly.

If you can, it is good to have everyone sitting in a circle or horseshoe. This gives an intimate feel. Obviously, if you are addressing 2000 people, a circle would be too large! It's OK in these circumstances to have straight rows. You can also have them sitting round small tables if you want to include a bit of group discussion. And that's not a bad idea.

How should the time be planned?

Plan your time carefully. If you have thirty minutes for your presentation, plan a couple of minutes for your warm-up, and about three to four minutes at the end to go over your main points again.

Write down your times for each part of the presentation and stick to them. There's nothing worse than a presentation that has to finish in mid-stream. Keep a wristwatch near your notes so you can have a crafty glance at it when you refer to your notes.

What materials do I need for the presentation?

Whatever you do, don't write it out word for word, and then read it. That is the quickest way to turn people off. On the other hand, you must rehearse what you want to say.

Write down a few headings on some cards and just glance at them so that you know what comes next. Put separate ideas on separate cards. You can also use transparencies, and those will then give the audience a map of your presentation.

It is best not to memorise your presentation, otherwise it can sound dry and unimaginative. However, do rehearse an opening that makes people sit up and listen.

How Do You Give Your Presentation Shape?

Similar to our advice when we looked at report writing, it is best to think of your presentation in three parts:

1 Tell 'em what you are going to tell 'em
2 Tell 'em
3 Tell 'em what you told 'em.

Give them the hors d'oeuvre

After a few brief introductory comments (and we mean brief), get onto the important things. The audience is not interested in apologies, details of traffic conditions or expressions of admiration for the wonderful facilities. And don't apologise for being a lousy speaker. It is guaranteed to make your audience believe that is exactly what you are.

Now explain what the purpose of your presentation is. You can do it with a snappy opener, something like: "If you implement my proposals, you will transform the work of your units within the next six months." Of course, it has to be true.

You don't have to start like that. You can begin with an interesting anecdote, but it must lead nicely into what you want to say. The important thing at this stage is that your audience must be convinced it is worth listening to you.

Next outline what you are going to say. Give them a map of the presentation. This helps them understand. Better still if you put it up on the screen.

Serve the main course

After the hors d'oeuvre comes the main course. Present your main points logically and simply.

This is the time when they will fall asleep or dream of the real main course! Don't try and feed them too much, therefore. Best to have just one or two points and to reinforce them by explaining them in different ways.

You can put the important points at the beginning, such as your recommendations. Why not? You may as well tell them while they are still conscious.

However, be careful if you have bad news. "I am going to explain to you how you will all lose your jobs within the next two years" is not the best way to start your presentation. You may find the dessert all over your face!

Finishing with the dessert

Earlier we said you have to plan your time. There is a good reason. For many of the audience, the only thing they will remember is what you say at the end. So if you run out of time and don't serve the 'dessert', they may remember nothing!

Repeat your main points and emphasise them. Go over the story again so that they see the full picture. And ensure you plan your final statement – it should be positive and leave them with an important thought to take away.

Finally, don't forget to thank them, even if they have been hostile and asked some rotten questions.

How Do You Make the Presentation Work Well?

Give it some sparkle

No one else can make the presentation interesting – only you. If you feel comfortable with it, use a bit of humour. The odd joke works wonders. But don't use humour in a destructive way, as a means of taking revenge on people.

Anecdotes also keep interest alive. The skill is in being able to relate what you say to the experiences of your audience. That way, you are guaranteed to be interesting.

Keep to the point

It's pretty easy to meander off course. But if you want your message to be understood, stay on track – from start to finish. That will keep it short. Some presenters are like gamblers: they don't know how to quit while they are ahead!

Don't try and be 'clever clogs'

Don't bamboozle people with technical jargon and long words. You should not be trying to impress your audience with your command of unintelligible vocabulary. Leave that to Sir Humphrey. Use short words and keep it simple.

Be your natural self

Don't think you are Sir John Gielgud. Be yourself. There is no need to stage manage smiles and gestures. Speak as you normally speak.

Set the tone

Tell yourself you like the audience, even if they are a load of #$%@s. It has quite an effect. It will make you smile and sound friendly. In return, they will almost certainly like you. If you appear too serious or aggressive, they will become resistant to what you have to say.

Keep the interest alive

Mention things they are familiar with, such as a name or an event. If they are strangers to you, all the more reason to do your homework. If you are addressing a handful of people, make sure you know their names, and refer to them. They will be pleased with that.

What should you wear?

Don't distract. Wear the clothes they expect you to wear. Being too casual can lower people's opinion of you – not very helpful if you are trying to be persuasive. So dress appropriately.

Don't just look at the smilers

Like most of us, you probably tend to look at people who smile supportively at you. They give you confidence. But also try to look at those who frown at you and shake their heads. And keep your enthusiasm up. It can infect even the cynics in your audience.

Open your mouth

Use your voice. Speak clearly and don't mumble. Vary your speed, emphasising the key words and phrases slowly. Also vary your tone. When we are nervous, we tend to speak in a monotone, which is far more effective than sleeping pills.

Don't flap your arms about

Don't pretend to be Andre Previn. A few gestures here and there are fine, but they should be natural. On the other hand, don't look like a tailor's dummy. A bit of movement at the right times can be good.

What Type of Presenter Are You?

Look at the speakers below. If you are one of these, you'd better rethink the way you do things.

♦ *"I'm sorry – this is not worth listening to . . ."*
He says this by apologising for his lack of knowledge and promising to waste as little of the audience's time as possible. He's right. He isn't worth listening to!

♦ *"I'm nervous and not enjoying this, so don't blame me."*
By not enjoying it, he is virtually ensuring the audience won't either. He is one of those for whom the ordeal is as welcome as an income tax demand, and he makes sure everyone knows.

♦ *"I'm bursting with energy . . ."*
And you are going to listen to him regardless. He covers about three days' material in 20 minutes flat.

♦ *"I'm rather fond of dancing."*
This person may do something which resembles a square tango

whilst trying to talk intelligently. All that's missing is the orchestra.

♦ *"I'd rather be a film star."*
This person dresses, speaks, moves and even looks like a film star. He regularly sweeps his hair back with his hand. He is more obsessed with his appearance than conveying a message. The audience is probably thinking, "Don't play it again Sam!"

♦ *"I have so much to say, I don't know where to start."*
This scatterbrained individual has no idea how to begin or end. Even his notes may be mixed up. He probably knows his stuff, but no one has a clue what he is talking about.

Finally . . .

How you put across your presentation determines whether it is instantly forgettable or well and truly imprinted on the mind. So it is no good just having something of monumental importance to say. You have to get your delivery spot on.

If you are going to present well, you have to put in the time getting it right. Only a fool pretends he can make a winning presentation without preparing.

Don't think you can be an overnight success. Expert presenters practise for hours on end. They work on their materials. They listen to themselves on tape. They watch themselves in the mirror. And they get feedback from their friends. It is only through such practice and preparation that you can achieve your goals.

How to Be an Expert Presenter

♦ Sort out the purpose of the presentation.
♦ Decide what you want your audience to take away.
♦ Plan your time and stick to it.
♦ Write down your main headings on cards or transparencies.
♦ Work out an interesting opener to gain the audience's attention.
♦ Repeat and re-emphasise your main points.
♦ Make the presentation to the point, simple, interesting and natural.
♦ Above all, do your homework and practise, practise, practise!

CHAPTER 20

Management Structure

Getting It Right

One of the amusing bits of fiction you can see when organisations show you their publicity materials is the organisation chart. You know what we mean: tree-like diagrams, some of them very long from top to bottom, maybe stretching over the bottom of the page, and others not so long but very, very wide.

The message is clear. The guy who sits on top of all this drives a smart 'Merc', whilst the chap on page 2 is lucky if he owns a bike.

You know these diagrams are real. After all, you are part of one, and almost certainly well up page 1. Why do we say fiction, then?

Nothing fictional, true, about the modes of transportation, but there is something not quite so accurate about these rather neat works of art.

Do They Always Work Out As Planned?

Seldom. They are supposed to work in particular ways, like Fred is obliged to report to Harry, and George can't ask Jim for three paper clips because there is no line drawn between their two names, which means it is not allowed. We suspect, nevertheless, that George makes clandestine overtures to Jim in order to get his paper clips.

It would be the chief executive's dream if organisational structures worked like they were meant to, but they don't, and that may not be a bad thing. We'll give you an example.

We were looking at an organisation that had a matrix structure (on paper, anyway). The organisation chart was a masterpiece of graphic art, suitable for London's Tate Gallery or an IQ puzzle book. There were lines all over the place, going in various directions and many of them

crossing one another. It wasn't clear who was at the top and the bottom, but the car park attendant looked pretty important. Quite right too!

This board game came with a set of instructions 'How to play'. They called them job descriptions. It appeared that everyone (spectators, visitors etc.) read them except the players themselves.

So the players made up their own rules. They did jobs they were *not* supposed to do and avoided jobs they *were* supposed to do. They talked to people they were *not* allowed to communicate with and ignored those they *were* supposed to work alongside.

To cut an epic down to manageable proportions, the organisation simply could not have worked without these activities. Things would not have got done; customers would not have been served.

The chart could not account for the fact that Bill, who was supposed to just manage the resources in his department, had years of contacts with neighbouring companies, and whenever they wanted anything, they called him. He was the expert. The guy who was supposed to deal with it (according to the plan) had no contacts, and was clueless about this part of the operation anyway.

There were plenty of stories like this one. Sometimes people got their hair off because others were not playing it 'by the book'. But, at least, the chief was astute. He knew about the real world, and that what was going on was in the organisation's best interests.

At one stage, he tried to match fact and fiction by changing the chart. Alas, nothing ever stays the same – different personnel, different customers, new products – so more fiction appeared. But it was a good attempt.

Putting the Pieces Together

The message from this is that there is often a difference between what is intended and what *really* goes on in an organisation. Charts seldom tell the true story. We would suggest that could be a good thing, and we shall explain why.

There is a management theory which talks about 'fit', that is matching what the organisation is trying to achieve with the things that go on in it. Using the jargon, the processes should be congruent with the strategies.

For example, suppose you want more people to travel by public transport and less by car. It would be silly to make bus fares expensive and petrol cheap.

Similarly, if you have an organisational strategy of arriving at innovative solutions, people who come up with creative ideas should be the ones to be rewarded, not those who can't see beyond the end of their noses.

Matching the Structure With What You Are Trying to Do

Also, according to this theory, structure too should be matched with strategy, although we doubt whether many organisations have ever thought of that. They tend to either do what others do, or institute something that looks nice on paper.

Just think, though – if you are in a volatile situation, things changing all the time, the chances are you should have a 'respond quick' type strategy. You probably need to accommodate customers' demands rapidly or they go elsewhere.

If your management structure slows down decision making and forces wide involvement whether it is relevant or not, the structure is out of tune with strategy.

Take this case. A local company contacted the neighbourhood college requiring some urgent computer training for its technicians. The matter was handed over to the Head of the Computer Section, who explained that he did not have authority to deal with this. He would refer it to the Head of Department, who would write a note to the Dean of School. The Dean would make his recommendation to the Deputy Director, who in turn would raise the matter at the next Board of Studies meeting in three months' time. See the problem?

The structures we set up have to be able to deal with our strategies effectively. As we said earlier, many organisations don't look at it from this point of view. They may do things the way they have always been done – they tend to get away with it if the environment is fairly stable – or they follow the fashion.

Complicated or Outdated Structures

One of these fashions was, and still is in some quarters, the matrix structure, seen for a time as the panacea for all structural ills.

Matrix structures are fine for some purposes and disastrous for others. They can lead to confusion, ambiguity and a great deal of unhappiness. In the right situation, they can make an organisation vibrant and responsive.

Holding on to outmoded structures may be as bad as implementing novel structures in the wrong situations. As we saw earlier, however, it may not matter too much if the 'real' activities compensate for the shortcomings. This is why we said it may not be a bad thing if the official chart tells lies.

Getting It Right

That is no excuse for letting things ride. Any senior manager must be concerned about getting it right. Your company's structure, for instance, should make it easy to get the right things done. It should help you, your seniors, peers and subordinates to be effective in their work – not obstruct them.

As one writer observes, if a business is well-managed and people are put in the right places, the formal structure and the informal goings on (what people actually do) will be identical.

If you are to be a skilful organisational designer, therefore, you have to incorporate the best bits of the informal networks in the formal pattern.

This means that structure has to be taken as seriously as the tasks, the information and decision processes, the reward system, and the selection of personnel to work in the system.

Don't think for one minute that you can deal with it by joining a few lines and boxes together in front of the TV one evening. A bad structure can cost you heaps of money.

What Sort of Structure Can You Have?

If you have any influence over the sort of structure your outfit uses, there are two extremes. One is the traditional bureaucratic structure and the other is a flexible, adaptive form.

Most of us have been subjected at some time or another to the bureaucratic nightmare, trying to get something done but the rules and regulations won't allow it.

Customer: Can you cash this cheque for me please?
Cashier: Sorry, but the bank's policy dictates that I have to ask for your identification.
Customer: Oh, come on, Freddie, I'm your mother!

Such conditions are certainly stifling and not very good at coping with the vagaries of present-day operating conditions for many businesses.

The basic problem with these is that there are too many layers. If you ask chiefs why they need so many management levels, they tell you all about span of control. In other words, one guy can control only so many. No one ever seems to question whether people need controlling. In some organisations, control, as these people think of it, only serves to constrain the work. So, before you talk about controlling people, consider whether that is what you really want.

Another related problem with old hierarchical structures is that territorial waters are guarded to the point of absurdity. Any encroachment is met with a twelve-bore shotgun. Not much use when you want collaboration.

The more flexible structures can adapt to the conditions, but they are not so good when things are quite stable. Indeed, the capricious adoption of matrix structures has led to even more difficulties in some organisations. Although the intention may have been good, they have often been expensive and confusing. So, you see, you can't have it both ways.

There are compromises, but you have to sort out what the organisation is about first. There is no point in designing some weird and wonderful structure because it looks good or because others are using it.

Some companies have skilfully used simple hierarchical forms (with not too many layers) and put integrating devices where they are needed. In other words, they have traditional big chiefs, middle bosses and workers. Each group of workers has one boss. But when a project is started, the rules can be broken. The project leader can legitimately tread on other bosses' territory, and, for that project, the workers have a new boss.

Some projects do cross the boundaries. This means that teams made up of people with different specialisms may be needed from time to time. There should be the facility to create them quickly when they are required.

This is very much in keeping with the advice given by Peters and

Waterman in their book *In Search of Excellence,* where they support the idea of using temporary forms to deal with cross-functional issues. They see simplicity as a feature that makes flexibility possible.

Go for Simplicity

That is an important word when we talk about structure. Our advice has always been to 'keep it simple'. Don't go in for complicated and unnecessary reporting relationships. Why should someone have to go through four or five people just to get permission to do something?

That sort of operation only serves to separate bosses from workers even more and make the pyramids taller. Yet, we are told by the experts we should be flattening them out.

Getting the Best of Both Worlds

It is true, there are many managers who will never let go. We saw this only too well in the first chapter. They hate to lose control. What is the way round this?

Managers can keep a hold on some things, but let people operate without interference on others. Groups and teams can play their own games, and because they understand their work, they can make their own decisions and respond quickly.

This way of structuring things has an enormous advantage over tightly controlled systems. Problems are localised. The chief executive does not have to lose sleep because your pen has run out of ink. People who are not involved don't have to waste time and energies on things that don't concern them.

What Can You Do to Improve Matters?

If it is right to free your organisation from the shackles of rigid central control, you need new sensitivities and ways of doing things. You have to rid your mind of narrow success indicators. You have to see that your employees may need to be creative and flexible. And you have to create conditions where your people can react quickly when things change.

There is more. You must communicate general direction, but accept that there are various ways of getting there. This means giving people meaningful work.

In terms of structure, therefore, centralise your organisation on certain key issues and stick rigidly to those – what its purpose is; what it should be doing; what its limits are; and who it should fight against. Everything else can be decentralised.

We are not talking of anarchy, where, if you get it wrong, no one takes notice of anyone else, failures are not put right and goals are not met. Nobody in his right mind wants that.

What we are advocating is giving people the freedom to be spontaneous and creative, yet retaining control of central values. The best of both worlds.

Start Small

You don't have to be the top bod in the organisation to be concerned with structure. You may be in charge of a small department, unit or section. You can certainly do something about the way you structure things there. And then, when it works well, who knows, you may be able to influence the larger organisation to get things operating more sensibly.

Accept That Things Have to Change

Of course, moving to a structure that enables things to get done means change, big change. Change, we all know, can be uncomfortable – literally:

> One guy working in an ultra-modern office, which had just installed the latest equally ultra-modern furniture, took a week to discover why he had suffered the most unbearable back pain – he had been sitting in the waste paper bin!

Change, nevertheless, may be essential. As we saw earlier, it is not always about putting people in boxes on a piece of paper and connecting them with neat lines. On the contrary, it may mean refocusing working procedures. It may mean converting paralysed departments into vibrant teams. It may also mean structuring meetings so that they solve problems rather than dwell on constraints. These are good starting points and they are at the heart of quality management.

Finally . . .

If organisational structures are to be removed from the fictional shelves, and if they are to support the key strategies, they may need to be thought about, not every fifty years, but on a frequent basis as part of the process of organisational review.

When strategy changes, so should the structure. It is only by ensuring that flexibility permeates the organisation that it can respond successfully to the dynamic challenges which typify our present-day world.

How to Get Your Management Structure Right

♦ Ensure your structure makes it easy to do the important things quickly and well.

♦ Keep it simple and understandable.

♦ The fewer the layers, the better.

♦ Centralise the key values, but let groups and teams make their own decisions on other things.

♦ Set the general direction, but free employees from rigid and stifling control.

♦ Above all, consider structure as flexible, something to be changed if strategies change.

Conclusion

Sometimes, when we get to the end of a book, we think "That's it! We know it all now". But, of course, that can never be true. Managers in this day and age can't afford to stop learning and searching for better ways of doing things. Chapter 1 pointed out only too well what happens when managers stagnate or refuse to develop. We hope, therefore, that you can view this book as a beginning, as a way of thinking about what you do now and how it can be improved.

The 'fabulous manager' is not perfect. But he tries. He constantly questions whether what he is doing is right and productive. In short, he genuinely does the best he can. That reminds us of a lovely de Mello story:

> "I find you guilty on forty-two counts and sentence you to two hundred and fifty-six years."
> The prisoner, an old man, was in despair. The judge, seeing this, softened his voice and said, "I know it sounds bad but I don't expect you to serve all of it."
> The old man, hearing this, looked up at the judge in hope.
> "Just do as much as you can," said the judge.

We can ask no more of you than to take managerial development seriously and to do just as much as you feel able.

Several themes may have become evident as you read through the chapters. These are of utmost importance, and we would now like to reinforce what we see as the keys to managerial success.

Most of what a manager does involves people. It involves working towards ways to assist them to improve performance, self-esteem, confidence and productivity. Managers who ignore the issues of feelings and motivation are unlikely to win any decorations from their staff.

Certainly, it is true we live in an age of mind-boggling technological advance, and companies who have the latest gadgetry can steal a jump on their competitors for a while. But the advantages don't last long and everything comes back to the human resource. Essentially, it is people who make the difference.

Another theme central to our book is that people need to keep growing and learning. There is little point in telling your staff they are important and valued if opportunities for development are not promoted and supported.

Empowerment, as we saw earlier, offers enormous scope for growth. If people can be involved in real decision making, and know their contributions are valued by management, they become tremendously valuable organisational assets.

Successful managers and organisations are able to share problems, successes and failures. They encourage people to comment on goals and strategies and to suggest improvements on how things are done.

Openness, of course, implies a more flexible approach to managing. The iron-fisted despot has a negligible role in today's organisation. Those who still insist on doing things that way, who dispense sterile orders like drinks from a machine, will find themselves slipping further and further behind the game.

That takes us to the final key, that of leadership. Much of what happens relates to leadership. When we write about people, empowerment and development, it is your role as a leader that is critical to success.

Managers today must be leaders, and we would suggest 'visible' ones. They need to be with and amongst their people, not on the periphery, pushing and pulling. They have to keep the vision in sight, promote excellence and truly involve their workers. We said earlier in the book that this isn't easy. Of course it isn't. Getting it right means higher levels of commitment than managers could realistically wish for.

The more reflective and skilled you become, the greater your ability to cope with the manager's role. The more you learn and grow, the better able you are to cope with changing responsibilities and circumstances. We hope that this short volume has provided the perspectives that might help you to become a more confident and competent manager, and that you can be described eventually by those who work for you as a 'fabulous manager'.

One final point. We have raised many issues and drawn on a range of theories in this book. Don't become intoxicated with them. And don't take the theory home every night. It can get out of hand:

> The wife asked her husband, who had just returned from a research methodology course in management: "How much do you love me?"
>
> He replied, "When you ask 'how much', are you referring to intensity, depth, frequency, quality or duration?"

We wish you a fruitful time in converting theory to practice.

Index

appraisal, 28, 89–96
  for determining pay, 91–2
  interviews, 94–5
  partnership, 92–3
assertiveness, in influencing, 119

Belbin, Meredith, 83–4

change, 9, 26, 45, 171
conflict, 133–40
  avoidance of, 135–8
  causes of, 133–5
  collaborative strategies in, 137–9
  compromise strategies in, 137
  positive and negative, 135
creativity, 9, 29, 62, 86, 135
culture, 9, 11, 34, 38, 49
  of high performance, 54

decentralisation, 171
decision making, 28, 30, 55,
  57–64, 167, 174
  acceptance, 61

experience, 62–3
  know-how, 60–1
  norms of, 63
  quality of, 61–2
  time for, 62
decisions, 36, 37, 50, 127
  by teams, 61–2
  types of, 58–60
delegation, 36, 65–73
  contract, 71
  task brief, 70
development, 20, 23, 25–30, 34,
  42, 53, 69, 70, 76-7, 91, 92, 174
  of individuals, 27–8
  manager's responsibility for,
    25–30
  in practice, 29–30
  of self, 26–7
  of teams, 28
  and training, 28–9

effectiveness, 10, 28
empowerment, 26, 27, 32-8, 174
excellence, 15, 92, 174
expectations, 53–4, 55, 68

halo effect, in interviewing, 101

influencing, 115–23
  strategies, 117–23
interviewing, 97–105
  questions, 101–3
interviews
  coordinated sets, 104
  location for, 98
  one-to-one, 103
  panel, 103–4
  preparation for, 98–9
  selection, 104–5

leader, 19, 33, 35, 37, 39–46
leadership, 19, 31, 37, 38, 39–46,
    174
  actions of, 44–5
  environment for, 42
  qualifications, 41
  qualities, 41
  style, 43–4, 46

management structure, 165–72
  bureaucratic, 168, 169
  flexible, 168, 169
  temporary forms, 170
  types of, 168–70
managers
  bad, 7–15
  good, 17–23
matrix structure, 168, 169
meetings, 125–31
  agendas, 129–30
  preparation for, 128–30
motivation, 12, 13, 27, 28, 45, 46,
    47–55, 92, 174
  in teams, 81

negotiation, 107–14
  preparing for, 110–1
  super agreements, 112–3
  tactics, 113–4

target, 110
threshold limit, 110

openness, 10, 13, 76, 79, 90–1,
    93, 174

Peters and Waterman, 169–70
planning, 28
policy, 21
presentations, 157–64
  preparation for, 158–60, 164
  structure of, 160–1
presenters, types of, 163–4
productivity, 25, 26, 27, 30, 36,
    37, 174

quality, Total Quality Management,
    8

reports
  accuracy, 154
  appearance, 151
  clarity, 152–3
  preparation, 150
  structure, 153–4
  style, 151–2
report writing, 149–55
reward, 10, 12, 35
risk taking, 37, 38, 82

self-development, 26
span of control, 169
structure, see management structure
supervision, 28
support, 52–3, 55

target setting, 28
team
  balance, 85–7
  culture, 81

team (*continued*)
  development, 28, 29, 30
  leadership, 81
  management, 22
  membership, 80
  process roles, 80, 83–7
  relationships, 78–9, 87
  size, 80
teamwork, 28, 75–82
time
  interruptions to, 145–6

  types of time thieves, 141–2
time management, 141–7
  communication, 144–5
  perfectionism, 144
  procrastination, 143
Total Quality Management, *see*
  quality
training, 28, 29, 30

vision, 35, 38, 45, 174

About the Authors

Kenneth Stott is a university lecturer with wide experience of leading development programmes for managers of all levels from both public and private sector organisations. Currently based in the UK at Middlesex University, he is a regular visitor to Southeast Asia where he worked for several years. With Allan Walker, he wrote *Making Management Work: A Practical Approach* which is used as a guide to effective management practice in many countries. He has also written regular feature articles on a range of management topics for the *Business Times* of Singapore. One of his major interests is in developing teamwork and much of his consultancy activity has been with organisations seeking to improve the quality and work of their teams.

Allan Walker has broad experience of teaching and research in management in Australia and Southeast Asia. He has worked in universities in the USA, Singapore and Australia, and is currently lecturing at Northern Territory University in Darwin. His main interests are in strategic planning, leadership, organisational teams and practical management skills. He is co-author and editor of several books and has published widely in international journals.